ERWIN CHEMERINSKY

A Court Divided

OCTOBER TERM 2023

ABA
AMERICAN BAR ASSOCIATION
Judicial Division

Cover design by ABA Design

Printed in the United States of America.

28 27 26 25 24 5 4 3 2 1

Library of Congress Cataloging-in-Publication Data

Names: Chemerinsky, Erwin, author. | American Bar Association. Judicial Division, issuing body.
Title: A court divided : October term 2023 / Erwin Chemerinsky.
Description: Chicago : American Bar Association, Judicial Division, 2025. | Includes index. | Summary: "A summary of the October 2023 completed Supreme Court term"— Provided by publisher.
Identifiers: LCCN 2024061816 (print) | LCCN 2024061817 (ebook) | ISBN 9781639055616 (paperback) | ISBN 9781639055623 (ebook)
Subjects: LCSH: United States. Supreme Court. | Constitutional law—United States. | United States. Constitution. 8th Amendment. | United States. Constitution. 1st Amendment.
Classification: LCC KF8742 .C463 2025 (print) | LCC KF8742 (ebook) | DDC 347.73/2609052—dc23/eng/20250111
LC record available at https://lccn.loc.gov/2024061816
LC ebook record available at https://lccn.loc.gov/2024061817

Discounts are available for books ordered in bulk. Special consideration is given to state bars, CLE programs, and other bar-related organizations. Inquire at Book Publishing, ABA Publishing, American Bar Association, 321 N. Clark Street, Chicago, Illinois 60654-7598.

www.shopABA.org

For my grandchildren,
Andrew, Sarah, and Amy

Contents

Preface

This is the fourth year in which I have the great pleasure of writing a book for the American Bar Association summarizing the just-completed Supreme Court term. I am grateful to Jeffrey Salyards at the ABA for making this possible and to Bob Edmunds and Herb Dixon for initially suggesting this series.

As I have said in past years, my goal in this book is to present the cases as clearly as I can and to explain their implications. My hope is to do this in a neutral manner, without evaluating them or editorializing. I certainly have views about many of them and cannot pretend that they do not sometimes affect my presentation of the cases. That is especially true about many of the cases this term—about presidential immunity, the administrative state, and the use of criminal law against the unhoused. My objective, though, is to present the cases as fairly as I can and leave my normative judgments to be expressed in other places.

I want to express my great appreciation to my research assistants—David Bernstein, Wyatt Singh, and Itai Tismanzky—for their terrific assistance. And as always, my wonderful executive assistant, Whitney Mello, was invaluable. Catherine Fisk and Alex Chemerinsky talked through many of the ideas in the book.

It was another very important term in the Supreme Court, and I feel privileged to have this opportunity to write about it.

1

Introduction

A Court Divided

By any standard, it was another momentous term in the U.S. Supreme Court. The Court decided 59 cases with signed opinions after briefing and oral argument. This seems to be the new normal for the Court. Each of the prior two years the Court decided 58 cases, the term before that it was 54, and the year before that it was 52, which was the smallest number since 1862. To put this in perspective, in the 1980s, the Court was deciding over 160 cases a year. The smaller docket began when William Rehnquist was Chief Justice. In his last term, October Term 2004, the Court decided 85 cases.

As the title for this book reflects, it is a deeply divided Court. At times, some have referred to the Supreme Court as "nine scorpions in a bottle."[1] That metaphor seems especially appropriate this year, though I would describe them as "nine angry scorpions."

There were a total of 59 opinions; 23 were 6–3 and another five were 5–4. Of course, the most apparent division was between the six conservative justices and the three liberal justices, and that split was crucial in some of the most important cases, particularly at the end of the term. These included decisions such as *Trump v. United States*[2] on presidential immunity, *Loper Bright Enterprises v. Raimondo*[3] and *Securities and Exchange Commission v. Jarkesy*[4] on the power of administrative agencies, and *City of Grants Pass v. Johnson*[5] on the ability of cities to use criminal laws against the unhoused.

Then there were the 6–3 decisions with Justices Clarence Thomas, Samuel Alito, and Neil Gorsuch in dissent, as they are now clearly the most conservative justices on a conservative Court. They, for example, vehemently dissented from the dismissal of an abortion case, *Moyle v. United States*,[6] and at the denial of standing in a case challenging the Biden administration's pressuring social media companies to take down false speech, *Murthy v. Missouri*.[7]

But even in cases where the Court was unanimous or nearly unanimous, there often were many different opinions. In *United States v. Rahimi*, the Court, 8–1, upheld a federal law prohibiting those under restraining orders in domestic violence cases from having guns.[8] But there were seven different opinions. There was serious debate among the conservative justices over the meaning and proper application of originalism as a method of constitutional interpretation. In *Moyle v. United States*, the Court dismissed the case as certiorari having been improvidently granted, but there were still seven different opinions.

Beyond all of this, there was the tone of many of the opinions. The justices often seemed angry, not just at the results, but with one another.

In terms of individual justices, this year showed that it is clearly the Roberts Court. John Roberts was in the majority more than any other justice, 96 percent of the time. He also wrote many of the most important opinions, including *Trump v. United States*, two crucial decisions restricting administrative agencies, and *United States v. Rahimi*.

It was a term when Justice Barrett's emerged as a distinctive voice. Occasionally, she joined the liberal justices, such as writing the dissent in *Fischer v. United States*, which involved a federal statute used in the January 6 insurrection prosecutions.[9] In several cases, such as *Rahimi* and *Vidal v. Elster* (a First Amendment case about whether the federal government can prohibit trademarks using a living person's name or likeness without consent), she wrote separately to elaborate her views about originalism.[10] In other notable cases, she wrote separately to offer a more moderate view than the other conservative justices, most notably in the two cases involving Donald Trump, *Trump v. Anderson* and *Trump v. United States*.[11] To be sure, she was with the conservatives in virtually every ideologically divided 6–3 decision, but her voice was notable this term.

Justice Thomas continued to write separately in a number of cases to urge the overruling of precedents.[12] Justice Alito seemed especially angry, particularly in some of his dissents.[13] Interestingly, Justice Alito wrote the fewest majority opinions of any justice, only four. Justices Sotomayor, Kagan, and Jackson each had occasions for writing blistering dissents.

An interesting but overlooked fact about the term is that of 59 decisions, only four were reviewing state court decisions. This has been the trend in recent years. In the prior two terms, only five cases in each were reviewing state court decisions. All of the rest come from federal courts of appeals.

An Overview

Here is a description of what I regard as some of the most important rulings of the term and how they reflected a Court divided, all of which are described in detail in subsequent chapters.

Abortion. For the first time since it overruled *Roe v. Wade* two years ago, the Court faced issues regarding the availability of abortions. Neither case involved a constitutional right to abortion, and neither was decided by the Supreme Court on the merits. In *Food and Drug Administration v. Alliance for Hippocratic Medicine*, the Supreme Court unanimously dismissed a lawsuit on standing grounds that challenged the FDA's rules that made mifepristone—a drug to induce abortions—more readily available.[14] In an opinion by Justice Brett Kavanaugh, the Court ruled that no plaintiff in the case could show an injury from the FDA's actions.

In *Moyle v. United States*, the Court dismissed certiorari as having been improvidently granted in a case that posed the issue of whether a federal statute—the Emergency Medical Treatment and Labor Act—which the Biden administration has interpreted to require abortions to protect the health of a pregnant person—preempts an Idaho law that allows abortions only to save someone's life.[15] Although the Court dismissed the case apparently on the grounds that the federal court of appeals had not yet ruled, there were four different opinions, and three justices (Alito, Thomas, and Gorsuch) dissented and would have ruled in favor of Idaho.

The administrative state. The term was especially important in the Court narrowing the powers of administrative agencies. In *Securities and Exchange Commission v. Jarkesy*, the Court, in a 6–3 decision authored by Chief Justice Roberts, held that it violates the Seventh Amendment right to jury trial for administrative agencies to impose civil penalties.[16] Justice Sonia Sotomayor wrote a strong dissent for the liberal justices, noting that this decision will affect the powers of over 200 agencies and lamenting the "Court's repeated failure to appreciate that its decisions can threaten the separation of powers."[17]

In one of the most high-profile decisions of the year, *Loper Bright Enterprises v. Raimondo*,[18] the Court overruled the 1984 decision *Chevron U.S.A. v. Natural Resources Defense Council*,[19] which held that federal courts should defer to federal agencies when they interpret ambiguous federal statutes. Chief Justice John Roberts wrote for the Court in a 6–3 decision and said that "the reviewing court—not the agency whose action it reviews—is to decide all relevant questions of law and interpret . . . statutory provisions."[20] Justice Elena Kagan wrote for the dissenting justices and said that this is likely to produce a "large scale disruption."[21] She explained that *Chevron* deference has been a crucial part of "modern government, supporting regulatory efforts of all kinds—to name a few, keeping air and water clean, food and drugs safe, and financial markets honest."[22]

Criminal law. In *City of Grants Pass v. Johnson*, the Court held, 6–3, that it does not violate the Eighth Amendment for a city to apply its anti-camping ordinances to criminally prosecute unhoused individuals for sleeping in public.[23] In an opinion by Justice Gorsuch, the Court reversed the Ninth Circuit, which held that it is cruel and unusual punishment for the government to punish people for sleeping in public when there are not adequate shelter beds. Justice Sotomayor wrote a blistering dissent and said that the decision means that for the homeless the message is "[e]ither stay awake or be arrested."[24]

In *Fischer v. United States*, the Court—again 6–3, but this time with Justice Barrett writing a dissent joined by Justices Sotomayor and Kagan—narrowed the scope of a federal law that had been used in the prosecution of individuals involved in the January 6 insurrection.[25] A provision of federal law, 18 U.S.C. § 1512(c)(1), makes anyone guilty of a felony who "otherwise obstructs, influences, or impedes any official proceeding, or attempts to do so." The Court said that this provision is narrow, and the government must establish that the defendant impaired, or attempted to impair, the availability or integrity of records, documents, objects, or other things used in an official proceeding. This case involved a defendant from the January 6 insurrection and will affect many convictions for actions on that day.

First Amendment. The most closely watched free speech case, *Moody v. NetChoice*, left undecided whether states can prohibit social media companies from engaging in content moderation.[26] In an opinion by Justice Elena Kagan, the Court said that this was a facial challenge to Florida and Texas laws, but the lower courts had not engaged in the proper analysis and sufficiently examined the full reach of the laws. Although the cases were remanded to the courts of appeals, the Court made clear that social media companies are private entities and generally have the First Amendment right to decide what to include or exclude on their platforms. This indicates a great likelihood that the state laws ultimately will be struck down, something that drew a strong disagreement in opinions by Justice Alito and Justice Thomas concurring in the judgment.

Second Amendment. In *United States v. Rahimi*, the Court upheld the constitutionality of a federal law that makes it a crime for a person under a restraining order in a domestic violence case to have a firearm.[27] The Court held that a person can be prohibited from having a gun "once a court has found that [the individual] represents a credible threat to the physical safety of another."[28]

Although it was an 8–1 decision, with only Justice Thomas dissenting, there were six opinions in the case. The Court adhered to its approach from *New York State Rifle and Pistol Association v. Bruen*,[29] that gun regulations are allowed only if supported by history and tradition. But the justices sharply disagreed on how a court should apply this originalist approach.

Donald Trump. In *Trump v. Anderson*, the Court ruled that Donald Trump was not disqualified from being elected president by Section 3 of the 14th Amendment.[30] In a per curiam opinion, the Court ruled that it is not for the states to enforce Section 3, but rather there must be a federal statute. Although the result was unanimous, Justices Sotomayor, Kagan, and Jackson filed an opinion concurring in the judgment that had the tone of a dissent. Justice Barrett wrote an opinion concurring in reasoning and in the judgment, chastising the liberal justices and saying, "[T]his is not the time to amplify disagreement with stridency. . . . Particularly in this circumstance, writings on the Court should turn the national temperature down, not up."[31]

Finally, in what many will regard as the most important case of the term, *Trump v. United States*, the Court broadly defined the scope of an ex-president's immunity from criminal prosecution.[32] In an opinion by Chief Justice John Roberts, the Court said that a president has absolute immunity for his official acts. The Court expansively defined this as anything done in carrying out the constitutional powers of the president or in implementing a federal statute. The conservative majority then went further and said that there is "at least a presumptive immunity from criminal prosecution for a president's acts within the outer perimeter of his official responsibility."[33] And Chief Justice Roberts said that a court cannot look at a president's motives.

Justices Sotomayor and Jackson each wrote blistering dissents. Justice Sotomayor explained the scope of the decision: "Orders the Navy's Seal Team 6 to assassinate a political rival? Immune. Organizes a military coup to hold onto power? Immune. Takes a bribe in exchange for a pardon? Immune. Immune, immune, immune."[34] Justice Sotomayor in her dissent says that the Court's decision, "in effect, completely insulate[s] Presidents from criminal liability."[35]

Ethics

It is impossible to discuss October Term 2023 without discussing the ethical issues that arose. The Supreme Court finally issued an ethics code for justices on Monday, November 13.[36]

The ethics code was accompanied by a prefatory statement: "The absence of a code, however, has led in recent years to the misunderstanding that the justices of this court, unlike all other jurists in this country, regard themselves as unrestricted by any ethics rules."[37] The statement said, "To dispel this misunderstanding, we are issuing this code, which largely represents a codification of principles that we have long regarded as governing our conduct."[38]

It is striking that the justices twice used the word "misunderstanding." Quite the contrary, the American people understood that every judge in the country—state and federal—was obligated to follow an ethics code except the most important judges: Supreme Court justices. Revelations of improprieties by several justices have contributed to the Court having its lowest approval rating in history.

Among other things, ProPublica, a nonprofit media organization, reported that Justice Thomas had failed to report many gifts from billionaires, including 38 vacations, 26 private flights, and stays at luxury resorts in Florida and Jamaica.[39] ProPublica also wrote that Harlan Crow had paid for some of Justice Thomas's vacations, including in Indonesia, and purchased from the Justice his mother's home. The *New York Times* reported that a wealthy friend forgave a substantial amount of a loan Justice Thomas had used to buy a quarter-million-dollar RV.[40] None of these matters was reported on the Justice's Financial Disclosure Reports as gifts or otherwise.

ProPublica reported Justice Samuel Alito took a luxury fishing trip with billionaire Paul Singer, whose hedge fund has repeatedly had business before the Court, without disclosing it.[41] Politico reported that Justice Neil Gorsuch sold real estate to the head of a law firm with business before the Court and did not disclose the purchaser's identity, in a 2017 transaction that took place days after Gorsuch was sworn in as a justice.[42] And the Associated Press reported that Justice Sotomayor's staff "prodded" schools and libraries to purchase her books when she was speaking there.[43]

All of this unquestionably explains why the Court finally adopted a code of ethics. Yet, it is important to recognize how it is weaker than the codes imposed on other judges in the country. A federal statute, 28 U.S.C. § 455(a), states:

> Any justice, judge or magistrate judge of the United States shall disqualify himself in any proceeding in which his impartiality might reasonably be questioned.

"Shall" is understood in the law as connoting a duty. But the ethics code for Supreme Court justices states that a justice "should disqualify himself or herself in a proceeding in which the Justice's impartiality might reasonably be questioned." It also uses the term "should" concerning the counterparts of circumstances in which the statute requires recusal, including, for example, when the Justice's "spouse . . . has an interest in the subject matter in controversy or in a party to the proceeding, or any other interest that could be substantially affected by the outcomes of the proceeding." "Should" is understood to mean that something is discretionary, not mandatory.

Moreover, the ethics code adopted by the Court leaves it entirely to each justice to decide whether to be disqualified in a particular case. In fact, a commentary following the ethics code says, "Individual justices, rather than the court, decide recusal issues."

The commentary to the rules discusses the problem for the Court when a justice is recused: there are only eight participating and there can be a tie. But this assumes that having nine justices participate is more important than ensuring compliance with ethical standards. It also ignores the reality that the Court often functions with eight justices when one is absent for illness or having been involved with the case previously in another court or when there is a vacancy. Republicans were unfazed by allowing a seat to remain open and having the Court with only eight justices after Antonin Scalia died in February 2016 until Neil Gorsuch was confirmed in April 2017.

There are many ways to handle recusal issues besides leaving it to each justice to decide for himself or herself. Jeremy Fogel, a former federal court judge and now the director of the Berkeley Judicial Institute, proposed to the Senate Judiciary Committee in May 2023 that the Chief Justice appoint three retired former federal court of appeals judges to decide recusal issues.[44] This is an elegant way of having recusals decided without involving the justices.

To be clear, it is better to have a code of ethics than to have none. But as with any law, a code of ethics is only meaningful if it is enforced.

There also were several ethical issues over the last year, especially concerning Justice Samuel Alito. Two incidents concern the display of flags outside Justice Alito's homes. On May 16, 2024, a *New York Times* article[45] revealed that in the days between the January 6, 2021, insurrection and President Joe Biden's inauguration, an upside-down American flag was flown outside Justice Alito's primary residence in Virginia. It is unknown how long the flag was displayed.[46] Although an upside-down American flag was historically used as a signal of distress, its presence outside the Alito residence raises ethical concerns because the upside-down flag has most recently become "a symbol of the 'Stop the Steal campaign,'" a movement by supporters of former President Trump urging Americans to falsely believe Joe Biden's election was the result of voter fraud.[47] Members of the Stop the Steal campaign were present at the January 6 insurrection, where they carried upside-down American flags.

On May 22, 2024, a second *New York Times* article reported on the display of an "Appeal to Heaven" flag outside Justice Alito's New Jersey beach home during the months of July, August, and September 2023.[48] It is unclear whether the flag was displayed continuously.[49] The display of an Appeal to Heaven flag poses similar ethical concerns to those posed by his flying of an upside-down American flag two years prior. Like upside-down American flags, Appeal to Heaven flags symbolize support for former President Trump.[50] Specifically, Appeal to Heaven flags represent "a religious strand of the 'Stop the Steal' campaign" that advocates "for a push to remake American [*sic*] government in Christian terms."[51]

On May 29, 2024, Justice Alito responded to a letter from Senators Richard Durbin and Sheldon Whitehouse requesting that Chief Justice Roberts ensure Justice Alito's recusal in *Trump v. United States* as well as any other cases relating to the 2020 presidential election or the January 6 insurrection.[52] Justice Alito wrote that he "had nothing whatsoever to do with the flying of [the upside-down American] flag" on his Virginia property, that he "was not even aware of the upside-down flag until it was called to [his] attention," that his wife had decided to fly the flag after enduring "numerous, loud, obscene, and personally insulting protests," and that he had asked his wife to "take it down" after becoming aware of it.[53] Justice Alito explained that due to his wife's joint ownership of their Virginia home, her First Amendment rights, and his respect for her as a person, he had no say as to the flag's display.[54] Justice Alito similarly attributed the Appeal to Heaven flag outside his New Jersey vacation home to his wife.[55] Justice Alito clarified: "My wife is fond of flying flags. I am not. . . . I was not familiar with the 'Appeal to Heaven' flag when my wife flew it. . . . I was not aware of any connection between this historic flag and the 'Stop the Steal Movement,' and neither was my wife."[56]

A potential ethical concern also arose out of Justice Alito's August 2023 sale of Anheuser-Busch stock worth somewhere between $1,000 and $15,000 and purchase of an amount of Molson Coors stock valued in the same range.[57] An article published on May 19, 2024, explained that "a manufactured, anti-transgender controversy" stemming from a transgender influencer's participation in a Bud Light March Madness campaign caused far-right and anti-LGBTQ conservatives to boycott both Bud Light and Bud Light's parent company, Anheuser-Busch. Justice Alito's sale of Anheuser-Busch and purchase of Molson Coors stock occurred during the same time period that boycotters traded Anheuser-Busch stock for shares in Molson Coors subsidiaries.[58] Although it is unknown whether Justice Alito bought and sold shares to participate in the boycott, the timing and substance of his behavior merit scrutiny because of the political nature of boycotts as well as his unusual position as "one of only two justices who currently own individual stocks."[59]

There also continued to be allegations of ethical improprieties concerning Justice Clarence Thomas. In June 2024, there were revelations that Justice Thomas took several more trips on the private plane of GOP megadonor Harlan Crow than were previously known. It was revealed that Thomas traveled on Crow's private jet during trips in 2017, 2019, and 2021 between various U.S. states.[60]

It is unclear how much the ethical issues contribute to the Court's having some of its lowest approval ratings in history[61] or whether they contribute to the rancor among the justices. But it is a set of issues concerning the Court this year that cannot be ignored.

Conclusion

Overall, October Term 2023 was another year of huge victories for conservative views. We saw again that the 2016 presidential election, which chose Donald Trump and led to his picking three Supreme Court justices, has led to dramatic changes in the law. We also saw that justices are frustrated with one another and that right now it is a very divided Court. Most of all, we saw—as the pages of this book detail—a Court that is significantly changing the law in a way that affects all of us and has a profound impact on American government and American society.

Endnotes

1. Noah Feldman, Scorpions: The Battles and Triumphs of FDR's Great Supreme Court Justices, at ii (2010).
2. Trump v. United States, 144 S. Ct. 2312 (2024) (discussed in Chapter 12).
3. Loper Bright Enters. v. Raimondo, 144 S. Ct. 2244 (2024) (discussed in Chapter 3).
4. Sec. & Exch. Comm'n v. Jarkesy, 144 S. Ct. 2117 (2024) (discussed in Chapter 3).
5. City of Grants Pass v. Johnson, 144 S. Ct. 2202 (2024) (discussed in Chapter 7).
6. Moyle v. United States, 144 S. Ct. 2015 (2024) (discussed in Chapter 2).
7. Murthy v. Missouri, 144 S. Ct. 1972 (2024) (discussed in Chapter 9).
8. United States v. Rahimi, 144 S. Ct. 1889 (2024) (discussed in Chapter 10).
9. Fischer v. United States, 144 S. Ct. 2176 (2024) (discussed in Chapter 6).
10. Vidal v. Elster, 602 U.S. 286 (2024) (discussed in Chapter 9).
11. Trump v. Anderson, 601 U.S. 100 (2024); Trump v. United States, 144 S. Ct. 2312 (2024) (discussed in Chapter 12).
12. *See, e.g.*, Food & Drug Admin. v. All. for Hippocratic Med., 602 U.S. 367, 398–99 (2024) (urging the overruling of cases allowing associational standing); City of Grants Pass v. Johnson, 144 S. Ct. 2202, 2234 (2024) (urging the overruling of *Robinson v. California*).
13. *See, e.g.*, Moyle v. United States, 144 S. Ct. 2015, 2027 (2024); Murthy v. Missouri, 144 S. Ct. 1972, 1997 (2024).
14. *Food & Drug Admin.*, 602 U.S. at 396–97 (discussed in Chapter 2).

15. *Moyle*, 144 S. Ct. at 2016 (discussed in Chapter 2).

16. Sec. & Exch. Comm'n v. Jarkesy, 144 S. Ct. 2117, 2139 (2024) (discussed in Chapter 3).

17. *Id.* at 2294.

18. Loper Bright Enters. v. Raimondo, 144 S. Ct. 2244, 2273 (2024) (discussed in Chapter 3).

19. Chevron U.S.A. Inc. v. Nat. Res. Def. Council, 468 U.S. 1227 (1984).

20. *Loper Bright Enters.*, 144 S. Ct. at 2265.

21. *Id.* at 2311 (Kagan, J., dissenting).

22. *Id.*

23. City of Grants Pass v. Johnson, 144 S. Ct. 2202, 2226 (2024) (discussed in Chapter 7).

24. *Id.* at 2228 (Sotomayor, J., dissenting).

25. Fischer v. United States, 144 S. Ct. 2176 (2024) (discussed in Chapter 6).

26. Moody v. NetChoice, 144 S. Ct. 2383 (2024) (discussed in Chapter 9).

27. United States v. Rahimi, 144 S. Ct. 1889, 1902 (2024) (discussed in Chapter 10).

28. *Id.* at 1902–03.

29. N.Y. State Rifle & Pistol Ass'n v. Bruen, 597 U.S. 1 (2022).

30. Trump v. Anderson, 601 U.S. 100, 106(2024) (discussed in Chapter 12).

31. *Id.* at 118 (Barrett, J., concurring).

32. Trump v. United States, 144 S. Ct. 2312, 2347 (2024) (discussed in Chapter 12).

33. *Id.* at 2331.

34. *Id.* at 2371 (Sotomayor, J., dissenting).

35. *Id.* at 2356.

36. *Code of Conduct for Justices of the Supreme Court of the United States* (Nov. 13, 2023), https://www.supremecourt.gov/about/Code-of-Conduct-for-Justices_November_13_2023.pdf.

37. *Id.*

38. *Id.*

39. Brett Murphy & Alex Mierjeski, *Clarence Thomas' 38 Vacations: The Other Billionaires Who Have Treated the Supreme Court Justice to Luxury Travel*, ProPublica (Aug. 10, 2023), https://www.propublica.org/article/clarence-thomas-other-billionaires-sokol-huizenga-novelly-supreme-court.

40. Jo Becker & Julie Tate, *Clarence Thomas's $267,230 R.V. and the Friend Who Financed It*, N.Y. Times (Aug. 5, 2023), https://www.nytimes.com/2023/08/05/us/clarence-thomas-rv-anthony-welters.html.

41. Justin Elliott, Joshua Kaplan & Alex Mierjeski, *Justice Samuel Alito Took Luxury Fishing Vacation with GOP Billionaire Who Later Had Cases*

before the Court, ProPublica (June 20, 2023), https://www.propublica.org/article/samuel-alito-luxury-fishing-trip-paul-singer-scotus-supreme-court#:~:text=The%20hedge%20fund%20was%20ultimately,according%20to%20ethics%20law%20experts.

42. Heidi Przybyla, *Law Firm Head Bought Gorsuch-Owned Property*, Politico (Apr. 25, 2023), https://www.politico.com/news/2023/04/25/neil-gorsuch-colorado-property-sale-00093579.

43. Brian Slodysko & Eric Tucker, *Supreme Court Justice Sotomayor's Staff Prodded Colleges and Libraries to Buy Her Books*, Associated Press (July 11, 2023), https://apnews.com/article/supreme-court-sotomayor-book-sales-ethics-colleges-b2cb93493f927f995829762cb8338c02.

44. *Senate Judiciary Committee Hearing on Supreme Court Ethics* (May 2, 2023), 1:40:30–1:41:10, https://www.c-span.org/video/?527741-1/senate-judiciary-committee-hearing-supreme-court-ethics.

45. Jodi Kantor, *At Justice Alito's House, a "Stop the Steal" Symbol on Display*, N.Y. Times (May 16, 2024), https://www.nytimes.com/2024/05/16/us/justice-alito-upside-down-flag.html.

46. *Id.*

47. *Id.*

48. Jodi Kantor et al., *Another Provocative Flag Was Flown at Another Alito Home*, N.Y. Times (May 22, 2024), https://www.nytimes.com/2024/05/22/us/justice-alito-flag-appeal-to-heaven.html.

49. *Id.*

50. *Id.*

51. *Id.*

52. Letter from Justice Samuel Alito to Senators Richard Durbin and Sheldon Whitehouse (May 29, 2024), https://www.judiciary.senate.gov/imo/media/doc/Letter%20from%20Justice%20Alito%20to%20Senators%20Durbin%20and%20Whitehouse.pdf.

53. *Id.*

54. *Id.*

55. *Id.*

56. *Id.*

57. Chris Geidner, *Exclusive: Justice Alito Sold Bud Light Stock amidst Anti-Trans Boycott Effort*, Law Dork (May 19, 2024), https://www.lawdork.com/p/alito-bud-light-stock-sale-anti-trans-boycott.

58. *Id.*

59. Chris Geidner, *An Alabama Trump Appointee Is Threatening to Jail LGBTQ Civil Rights Lawyers*, Law Dork (May 21, 2024), https://www.lawdork.com/p/alabama-burke-threatening-jail-lgbtq-lawyers?open=false#§more-about-alito.

60. Tierney Sneed & John Fritze, *Justice Clarence Thomas Took More Trips on GOP Megadonor's Private Plane Than Previously Known*, CNN (June 13, 2024), https://www.cnn.com/2024/06/13/politics/clarence-thomas-harlan-crow-private-plane-ethics-supreme-court/index.html.

61. Olivia Alafriz, *Supreme Court's Approval Rating Ticks Up, Poll Shows*, POLITICO (Apr. 3, 2024), https://www.politico.com/news/2024/04/03/supreme-court-approval-ratings-00150365.

2

Abortion

Quite predictably, the Court's decision in 2022 in *Dobbs v. Jackson Women's Health Organization*,[1] overruling *Roe v. Wade*,[2] has led to the passage of laws in many states that greatly restrict abortion. It also has led to a large amount of litigation involving a myriad of issues regarding access to abortion.

In the October Term of 2023, the Court, for the first time since *Dobbs*, had two cases concerning abortion. Neither case, of course, concerned whether there is a constitutional right to abortion; that was resolved in *Dobbs*. But both cases had the potential to greatly affect the availability of abortions in the United States. In neither, though, did the Court decide the legal issues presented. In one the Court dismissed based on standing, and in the other the Court dismissed the case altogether as certiorari having been improvidently granted. The issues presented, which could matter greatly for abortion in the United States, remain unresolved.

Food and Drug Administration v. Alliance for Hippocratic Medicine

In 2000, the Food and Drug Administration (FDA) approved a two-drug protocol for medically induced abortion using mifepristone and misoprostol. According to the Guttmacher Institute, in 2023, about 63 percent of all abortions were medically induced, rather than surgically performed. This makes the availability of these drugs enormously important. Also, especially in states where abortions are illegal and no doctor will perform them, the ability of a woman to take pills to induce an abortion takes on great significance.

The Alliance for Hippocratic Medicine, represented by the Alliance Defending Freedom, a conservative Christian organization, brought a challenge to the FDA's approval of mifepristone. The challengers claim that the FDA improperly used an accelerated approval process for mifepristone that is reserved for new drugs that would benefit patients with serious or life-threatening illnesses.

The challengers intentionally filed their case in the Amarillo Division of the U.S. District Court for the Northern District of Texas because there is only one judge, Matthew Kacsmaryk, in that division and every case filed there goes to him.

President Donald Trump appointed Kacsmaryk, who had been deputy general counsel to the very conservative First Liberty Institute. He was known to be a strong opponent of abortion rights. Kacsmaryk, in his ruling, did not disappoint the challengers to mifepristone; he could not have been clearer in his hostility to abortion rights.[3] He said that the drug exists "to kill the unborn human."[4] Indeed, Judge Kacsmaryk explained why he believed using the term "fetus" is inaccurate while the terms "unborn human" or "unborn child" are appropriate.[5] He then went even further in suggesting that the embryo has legal rights, something no court ever has espoused and that antiabortion groups surely will seize on in trying to argue that laws allowing abortion are unconstitutional.

Kacsmaryk found that the FDA abused its discretion in approving mifepristone. This was the first time a judge ever has overturned the FDA's approval of a drug. He did so even though the drug has been on the market for 23 years and has been repeatedly proven to be safe and effective. Medically induced abortions are safer than surgical abortions and far safer than childbirth. Evidence before the court showed that complications from mifepristone occur at a lower rate than that seen with wisdom teeth removal, colonoscopies, and other routine medical procedures.[6] Kacsmaryk repeatedly disagreed with the judgment of the FDA, relying on the literature from antiabortion groups, including the unfounded claim that many women regret their abortions. Kacsmaryk issued a nationwide injunction preventing the distribution of mifepristone anywhere in the country.

A conservative panel of the U.S. Court of Appeals for the Fifth Circuit in part reversed and in part affirmed.[7] Although the Fifth Circuit said that the district court was wrong in stopping all use of mifepristone after it had been on the market for 23 years, the appellate court overturned fairly recent FDA actions to make the drug more easily available. In 2016, the FDA said that the drug could be used until the tenth week of pregnancy rather than just to the seventh week, reduced the number of required in-person clinical visits from three to one, and allowed nonphysician healthcare providers licensed under state law to prescribe and dispense drugs, such as nurse practitioners, to prescribe and dispense mifepristone. It also reduced the dosage from 600 mg to 200 mg. In 2021, the FDA eliminated the requirement that mifepristone be administered in person; it was the only drug where there was such a requirement. But the Fifth Circuit overturned these 2016 and 2021 changes, concluding that they were "arbitrary and capricious" on the part of the FDA.[8]

The U.S. Supreme Court unanimously reversed the Fifth Circuit on standing grounds.[9] Justice Brett Kavanaugh wrote the opinion for the Court. In order to sue in federal court, a plaintiff must show that he or she is personally injured by the action being challenged, that the harm is caused by the defendant, and that a favorable federal court decision would remedy the injury. The Supreme Court long has said that Article III of the Constitution, which creates the federal judiciary and defines its powers, imposes these requirements for standing to sue in federal court.

The Court dismissed the challenge to mifepristone for lack of standing, concluding: "But the plaintiffs do not prescribe or use mifepristone. And FDA is not requiring them to do or refrain from doing anything. Rather, the plaintiffs want FDA to make mifepristone more difficult for other doctors to prescribe and for pregnant women to obtain. Under Article III of the Constitution, a plaintiff's desire to make a drug less available *for others* does not establish standing to sue."[10]

At the oral arguments before the Court in March, the attorney for the plaintiffs, Erin Hawley, said that there could be an injury if mifepristone failed to induce an abortion and an emergency room doctor who opposed abortion had to then perform one. The justices asked her if that had ever happened, and she could not point to a single example. As Justice Kavanaugh pointed out in his opinion, not only is the "FDA [] not requiring [doctors] to do or refrain from doing anything,"[11] but federal law also protects doctors from having to perform procedures that violate their conscience. Justice Kavanaugh noted that "plaintiffs have not shown—and cannot show—that FDA's actions will cause them to suffer any conscience injury."[12]

The challengers also argued that doctors would be hurt because women suffering complications from mifepristone would be likely to burden emergency rooms. But the Court rejected that as insufficient for standing and said: "[T]he law has never permitted doctors to challenge the government's loosening of general public safety requirements simply because more individuals might then show up at emergency rooms or in doctors' offices with follow-on injuries. Stated otherwise, there is no Article III doctrine of 'doctor standing' that allows doctors to challenge general government safety regulations. Nor will this Court now create such a novel standing doctrine out of whole cloth. Consider some examples. EPA rolls back emissions standards for power plants—does a doctor have standing to sue because she may need to spend more time treating asthma patients? . . . The answer is no: The chain of causation is simply too attenuated."[13]

The Court's decision is a relief for those who support abortion rights and for the many pregnant individuals who will continue to have mifepristone available to induce abortions before the tenth week of pregnancy. But there are other lawsuits pending that challenge the approval of mifepristone.[14] It is unclear as to who, if anyone, will have standing to challenge the FDA's actions.

During the same oral arguments in March, two justices raised an 1873 statute, the Comstock Act, which could threaten the availability of mifepristone. The Comstock Act was adopted in 1873 to prohibit the shipment of obscene materials through the mails, including, at the time, "any article or thing designed or intended for the prevention of conception or procuring of abortion." As the Supreme Court explained, antivice crusader

Anthony Comstock successfully lobbied Congress and state legislatures in the 19th century to enact expansive laws "to prevent the mails from being used to corrupt the public morals."[15]

The current version of the Comstock Act still prohibits the shipment through the mails of "[e]very article or thing designed, adapted, or intended for producing abortion." It also forbids any "express company or other common carrier" from providing for "carriage" of such items "in interstate or foreign commerce."[16] The act provides for a sentence of up to five years for the first offense and ten years for the second offense plus a fine.

For over a century, courts have given a narrow construction to the Comstock Act, and it has not been used. The U.S. Department of Justice in an opinion memorandum in December 2022 said that the Comstock Act had been interpreted to apply only to the intentional unlawful shipping of articles intended to produce abortions. The opinion concluded: "Because there are manifold ways in which recipients in every state may lawfully use such drugs, including to produce an abortion, the mere mailing of such drugs to a particular jurisdiction is an insufficient basis for concluding that the sender intends them to be used unlawfully."[17]

But the Justice Department's opinion is not binding on any court or on a future presidential administration. A future Justice Department could criminally prosecute shipping drugs or hold that anything mailed that can produce abortion violates the terms of the Comstock Act. This would effectively end abortions by medication. Any shipment of the drugs would be deemed a violation of federal law.

The point is that the Supreme Court in *Food and Drug Administration v. Alliance for Hippocratic Medicine* dismissed the challenge to mifepristone on standing grounds without granting or denying the drug any further protection. The efforts by antiabortion groups to ban it can and will continue.

Moyle v. United States

The Court decided even less in *Moyle v. United States*, dismissing the petition for certiorari as improvidently granted.[18] Interestingly, although the Court dismissed the case, there were four separate opinions that gave a clear sense of the views of some of the justices.

The Emergency Medical Treatment and Labor Act (EMTALA) requires a Medicare-funded hospital to provide essential care to patients experiencing medical emergencies. The Biden administration has interpreted EMTALA as requiring that Medicare-funded hospitals offer abortions when needed to stabilize medical conditions that seriously threaten a pregnant woman's life or health.[19]

However, Idaho prohibits abortion except if necessary to save the life of the woman. A federal district court found that the Idaho law is likely preempted in situations where federal law would require that an abortion be performed to protect the health of the patient, but state law would forbid it.[20] The district court issued a preliminary injunction. The Ninth Circuit, en banc, declined to stay the injunction. Idaho sought emergency relief from the Supreme Court, and the Court responded by granting certiorari and having briefing and oral arguments.

But the Court then dismissed the case without a decision. As is done in such circumstances, the Court simply issues a one-sentence order that certiorari was improvidently granted. The matter returns to the Ninth Circuit. Nonetheless, there were four separate opinions.

Justice Elena Kagan, joined by Justices Sotomayor and Jackson, said that "Idaho's arguments about EMTALA do not justify, and have never justified, either emergency relief or our early consideration of this dispute."[21] Nonetheless, Justice Kagan made clear that she believes that the Idaho law is preempted. Federal law requires that abortions be provided to protect a woman's health or life, while Idaho law prohibits abortions except if needed to save the woman's life. In a situation where a woman goes to an emergency room and her health, including her future reproductive health, would be in jeopardy without an abortion, federal law would require one to be performed, but Idaho law would forbid it unless necessary to save her life. Justice Kagan wrote: "Because the Idaho law conflicts with that requirement—prevents hospitals from doing what EMTALA commands—the Court is right to dissolve its stay of the District Court's injunction. Doing so will again give Idaho women access to all the needed medical treatments that EMTALA guarantees."[22]

Justice Jackson wrote an opinion concurring in part and dissenting in part. She would have made explicit that the Idaho law is preempted. She wrote: "[T]he conflict between the state and federal law—as they are actually being interpreted and applied on the ground—is both substantial and significant. . . . Put simply, under federal law, a hospital *must* provide an emergency abortion that is reasonably necessary to preserve a patient's health within the meaning of EMTALA. But, under Idaho law, a doctor cannot provide this care (required by federal law) without committing a criminal act."[23] Justice Jackson was forceful in her disagreement and declared: "There is simply no good reason not to resolve this conflict now."[24]

Justice Barrett, joined by Chief Justice Roberts and Justice Kavanaugh, wrote a concurring opinion and said that the Court erred by granting certiorari before there was a decision from the court of appeals.[25] She noted that there had been changes in the positions both of the federal government as to the meaning of EMTALA and of Idaho as to the scope of its law. Especially in light of this, she said that the case should return to the Ninth Circuit before the Supreme Court takes up the issue.

Justice Alito wrote an angry dissent, joined by Justices Thomas and Gorsuch.[26] The dissenting justices would have had the Court decide the merits and hold that the Idaho law is not preempted. Justice Alito wrote: "The Government's preemption theory is plainly unsound. Far from requiring hospitals to perform abortions, EMTALA's text unambiguously demands that Medicare-funded hospitals protect the health of both a pregnant woman *and* her 'unborn child.' And even if there were some ambiguity in the statutory text, we would be obligated to resolve that ambiguity in favor of the State because EMTALA was enacted under the Spending Clause, and as we have held time and again, conditions attached to the receipt of federal funds must be unambiguous."[27]

The Court thus leaves unresolved whether state laws prohibiting all abortions except when needed to save the life of the pregnant person are preempted by EMTALA when an abortion would protect the health of the woman. The issue is sure to return to the Court. It is apparent that there are three justices—Kagan, Sotomayor, and Jackson—who will find preemption and three justices who reject the preemption argument: Alito,

Thomas, and Gorsuch. That leaves Barrett, Roberts, and Kavanaugh, and they give no indication of how they will decide.

Justice Alito is angry that the Court did not rule in favor of Idaho. And Justice Jackson is just as angry that the Court did not find the Idaho law preempted. She wrote:

> So, to be clear: Today's decision is not a victory for pregnant patients in Idaho. It is delay. While this Court dawdles and the country waits, pregnant people experiencing emergency medical conditions remain in a precarious position, as their doctors are kept in the dark about what the law requires. This Court had a chance to bring clarity and certainty to this tragic situation, and we have squandered it. And for as long as we refuse to declare what the law requires, pregnant patients in Idaho, Texas, and elsewhere will be paying the price.[28]

The one thing that is certain is that this issue, and many others concerning abortion that are now being litigated in the lower courts, will return to the U.S. Supreme Court. Overruling *Roe* did many things, but it did not lessen—and actually increased—litigation over abortion issues.

Endnotes

1. Dobbs v. Jackson Women's Health Org., 597 U.S. 215, 142 S. Ct. 2228 (2022).
2. Roe v. Wade, 410 U.S. 113, 93 S. Ct. 705 (1973).
3. All. for Hippocratic Med. v. U.S. Food & Drug Admin., 668 F. Supp. 3d 507 (2023).
4. *Id.* at 521.
5. *Id.* at 520 n.1.
6. Brief for Medical & Public Health Societies as Amici Curiae Supporting Respondents at 9–10, All. for Hippocratic Med. v. U.S. Food & Drug Admin., 668 F. Supp. 3d 507 (N.D. Tex. 2023) (No. 2:22-CV-223-Z).
7. All. for Hippocratic Med. v. Food & Drug Admin., No. 23-10362, 2023 WL 2913725 (5th Cir. 2023).
8. *Id.* at *17.

9. Food & Drug Admin. v. All. for Hippocratic Med., 144 S. Ct. 1540 (2024).

10. *Id.* at 1552.

11. *Id.*

12. *Id.* at 1561.

13. *Id.* at 1562.

14. *See, e.g.*, Bryant v. Stein, No. 1:23-CV-77, 2024 WL 1886907 (M.D.N.C. 2024); Whole Woman's Health All. v. Food & Drug Admin., No. 3:23-CV-00019, 2023 WL 5401885 (W.D. Va. 2023).

15. Bolger v. Youngs Drug Prods. Corp., 463 U.S. 60, 103 S. Ct. 2875, 2882 n.19 (1983).

16. 18 U.S.C. §§ 1461, 1462.

17. Memorandum from the Justice Department to the General Counsel of the United States Postal Service, Application of the Comstock Act to the Mailing of Prescription Drugs That Can Be Used for Abortions (Dec. 23, 2022).

18. Moyle v. United States, 144 S. Ct. 2015 (2024).

19. 42 U.S.C. § 1395dd.

20. United States v. Idaho, 623 F. Supp. 3d 1096 (D. Idaho 2022).

21. *Moyle*, 144 S. Ct. at 2017.

22. *Id.* at 2019.

23. *Id.* at 2024.

24. *Id.* at 2026.

25. *Id.* at 2019.

26. *Id.* at 2027.

27. *Id.* at 2027–28.

28. *Id.* at 2027.

3

Administrative Law

The most significant change in American government since 1787 has been the creation of a myriad of administrative agencies that affect literally every aspect of life and society. Federal agencies have existed since the beginning of the country, but they increased in the late 19th and early 20th centuries, exploded in number and authority in the New Deal, and continued to increase since then.

In the last few years, the Roberts Court has dramatically changed administrative law and is very much in the process of remaking the administrative state. In the prior two terms, the Court created a new doctrine to limit the power of federal agencies: the major questions doctrine. This is the principle that a federal agency cannot act on a major question of economic or political significance unless it has clear direction from Congress. The Court applied this doctrine to hold that the Environmental Protection Agency (EPA) lacks authority to regulate greenhouse gas emissions from coal-fired power plants[1] and that the Secretary of Education lacked authority to adopt a loan forgiveness program.[2] This has spawned a great deal of litigation over what is a major question and what is sufficient congressional guidance to allow an agency to act.

In October Term 2023, the Supreme Court, in a series of decisions, significantly changed administrative law, overall reducing the power of federal agencies and increasing the authority of courts over them. The

Court did this, as discussed later, by overruling the *Chevron* doctrine,[3] by precluding agencies from imposing monetary penalties,[4] and by significantly expanding the time for challenging an agency action.[5]

Each of these developments individually is significant for judges, lawyers, and the law. Cumulatively they are bringing about a radical change in government. Each of these cases over the last few terms has been a 6–3 decision, with the justices ideologically divided.

The administrative state has been based on the premise that Congress may create federal agencies with broad authority to implement the law, that it is unrealistic for Congress to legislate in great detail and that it needs to leave much to the agencies, and that the agencies have expertise to which courts should defer. The liberal justices on the Court continue to accept these premises. But the conservative justices clearly reject them, and their decisions reflect a desire to have more extensive judicial limits and control over agency powers.

Why is there this ideological divide? Some of it may be that the conservatives are generally quite pro-business, and businesses, for obvious reasons, oppose regulations and want more opportunity for courts to overturn agency decisions. Some of it may be a loss of faith in the idea of expertise, especially by conservatives, something we see in other parts of society as well. Some of it may be the influence of the formalism and originalism of the conservative justices. Federal agencies and their powers do not easily fit into the structure of the Constitution created in 1787.

The bottom line is that the administrative law decisions of this term are a major change in the law and part of a larger trend from the Roberts Court.

The End of *Chevron* Deference

In 1984, in *Chevron U.S.A. v. Natural Resources Defense Council*, the Supreme Court unanimously held that federal courts should defer to federal agencies when they interpret ambiguous federal statutes so long as their interpretation is reasonable.[6] *Chevron* prescribed a two-step inquiry. First, a court determines whether the federal statute is clear. Only if the answer is no and the statute is ambiguous does the court move to the second step and defer to the agency's interpretation if it is based on a permissible, and reasonable, construction of the law.

For example, the Clean Air Act gives the EPA the authority to regulate how much of certain pollutants can be emitted into the air. *Chevron* deference means that a court should defer to the reasonable judgment of the EPA when it adopts rules for how much of a pollutant can be put into the air. *Chevron* deference is based on the idea that Congress cannot legislate with specificity for every matter and desires to leave many matters to the expertise of the federal agency. Especially with regard to technical matters, the agencies and not the courts are the experts.

Loper Bright Enterprises v. Raimondo, and its companion case, *Relentless v. Department of Commerce*, involved a federal statute—the Magnuson-Stevens Fishery Conservation and Management Act—that gives management authorities over fisheries to the National Marine Fisheries Service, an agency housed under the Department of Commerce's National Oceanic and Atmospheric Administration. As a way of ensuring compliance with its rules, the service required observers to be on board certain fishing boats. Specifically, the case involved a requirement of observers on herring boats. Fishing companies brought a challenge, and the lower courts ruled against them, invoking *Chevron* deference.[7]

The Supreme Court used this as the occasion for expressly overruling *Chevron*.

The Court was explicit and said that "the reviewing court—not the agency whose action it reviews—is to decide all relevant questions of law and interpret . . . statutory provisions."[8] Interestingly, the Court began its analysis by focusing on the need for courts to make independent judgments, invoking *Marbury v. Madison*.[9] The Court referred to the "elemental proposition reflected by judicial practice dating back to *Marbury*: that courts decide legal questions by applying their own judgment."[10]

The Court said that, under the Administrative Procedure Act, it is for courts to decide questions of law and that *Chevron* deference cannot be reconciled with the proper role of the judiciary. Chief Justice Roberts stated: "Perhaps most fundamentally, *Chevron*'s presumption is misguided because agencies have no special competence in resolving statutory ambiguities. Courts do. The Framers, as noted, anticipated that courts would often confront statutory ambiguities and expected that courts would resolve them by exercising independent legal judgment."[11] The Court thus concluded its opinion: "*Chevron* is overruled. Courts must exercise their independent judgment in deciding whether an agency has acted within its statutory authority, as the APA requires."[12]

Justice Gorsuch wrote a lengthy concurring opinion, while Justice Kagan wrote an angry dissent, joined by Justices Sotomayor and Jackson, and said that overruling *Chevron* is likely to cause a "large scale disruption."[13] Justice Kagan invoked stare decisis and objected to the overruling of a 40-year-old precedent, especially because Congress could have amended the Administrative Procedure Act to eliminate *Chevron* deference if it wished to do so. She said that *Chevron* deference has been a crucial part of "modern government, supporting regulatory efforts of all kinds—to name a few, keeping air and water clean, food and drugs safe, and financial markets honest."[14]

Justice Kagan argued that Congress intended judicial deference to the expertise of administrative agencies. She said that a "rule of judicial humility gives way to a rule of judicial hubris."[15] She concluded: "All that backs today's decision is the majority's belief that *Chevron* was wrong—that it gave agencies too much power and courts not enough. But shifting views about the worth of regulatory actors and their work do not justify overhauling a cornerstone of administrative law. In that sense too, today's majority has lost sight of its proper role."[16]

Overruling *Chevron* deference means that it will be easier for courts to overturn and delay agency actions. The result will be many more challenges to agencies in federal courts, requiring judges to wade through the details of complex federal regulations. Again, it is the Court limiting the authority of federal agencies and increasing the power of the courts.

Civil Penalties

The Court limited agency power in another way: it held for the first time that federal agencies may not impose civil penalties. In *Securities and Exchange Commission v. Jarkesy*, the Court ruled that the Seventh Amendment right to jury trial requires that civil penalties, at least for fraud claims, be brought to federal court.[17] As Justice Sotomayor pointed out in a dissent, there "are more than 200 statutes authorizing dozens of agencies to impose civil penalties for violations of statutory obligations."[18] This is thus a major curtailment of agency power.

The Securities and Exchange Commission (SEC) has the authority to seek civil penalties in administrative proceedings (which ultimately can be reviewed in a court) or in a federal district court. A jury trial is available in court, but not in an agency.

The SEC launched an investigation against George Jarkesy and his company, Patriot28. The SEC chose to proceed in an administrative proceeding before an administrative law judge. There was a finding against Jarkesy and his company. The SEC reviewed the decision and issued a final order that levied a civil penalty of $300,000 against Jarkesy and Patriot28, directed them to cease and desist committing or causing violations of the antifraud provisions, ordered Patriot28 to disgorge earnings, and prohibited Jarkesy from participating in the securities industry and in offerings of penny stocks.

The Supreme Court, in a 6–3 decision, found that the administrative proceedings violated the Seventh Amendment. Chief Justice Roberts wrote for the majority and declared: "This case poses a straightforward question: whether the Seventh Amendment entitles a defendant to a jury trial when the SEC seeks civil penalties against him for securities fraud. The threshold issue is whether this action implicates the Seventh Amendment. It does. The SEC's antifraud provisions replicate common law fraud, and it is well established that common law claims must be heard by a jury."[19] The Court stressed, under an originalist and history focused analysis, that fraud was a type of claim that was heard by juries in England and at common law in the United States, so the SEC's claim similarly required a jury trial.

The Court acknowledged that there is a doctrine for "public rights" that allows Congress to assign some matters to agencies rather than Article III courts. The effect, of course, is that there is not a jury trial available in the agency. Prior cases indicated that public rights matters are those between the government and private parties.[20] But the Court rejected this broad definition of public rights. It said instead: "The Constitution prohibits Congress from 'withdraw[ing] from judicial cognizance any matter which, from its nature, is the subject of a suit at the common law.'

Once such a suit 'is brought within the bounds of federal jurisdiction,' an Article III court must decide it, with a jury if the Seventh Amendment applies. These propositions are critical to maintaining the proper role of the Judiciary in the Constitution."[21]

Chief Justice Roberts made clear that this case was not only about the Seventh Amendment, but also about separation of powers. He concluded his majority opinion: "A defendant facing a fraud suit has the right to be tried by a jury of his peers before a neutral adjudicator. Rather than recognize that right, the dissent would permit Congress to concentrate the roles of prosecutor, judge, and jury in the hands of the Executive Branch. That is the very opposite of the separation of powers that the Constitution demands."[22]

Justice Sotomayor wrote a scathing dissent, joined by Justices Kagan and Jackson. She stressed that this was the first time that the Court ever had imposed this limit on Congress and federal agencies. She explained that Congress long has had the authority to assign disputes between the government and private parties to federal agencies where there is not a right to trial by jury. She said the Court was "plainly wrong. This Court has held, without exception, that Congress has broad latitude to create statutory obligations that entitle the Government to civil penalties, and then to assign their enforcement outside the regular courts of law where there are no juries."[23]

Justice Sotomayor identified over two dozen agencies that have statutory power to impose penalties in agency proceedings. For some, there is no statutory authority to go to court. She was blunt in saying: "Make no mistake: Today's decision is a power grab. Once again, the majority arrogates Congress's policymaking role to itself. . . . Judicial aggrandizement is as pernicious to the separation of powers as any aggrandizing action from either of the political branches."[24]

There are a number of questions left unanswered by the Court's decision in *Jarkesy*. First, can agencies ever impose civil penalties? The Court's opinion stresses that they cannot do so for fraud. But that leaves open whether it will be permissible for any other type of claim. Second, what about agencies that don't have the statutory authority to bring court proceedings? Will it take an act of Congress for these agencies to be able to recover civil penalties? Third, what will this mean for the public rights doctrine and the ability of non–Article III courts to hear other matters? I always understood the public rights doctrine to be about congressional power to place disputes between the government and private parties into agencies or non–Article III courts.[25] But the Court in *Jarkesy* has a narrower view of the public rights doctrine, the contours of which are not clear.

Statute of Limitations for Challenges to Agency Actions

The issue in *Corner Post v. Board of Governors of the Federal Reserve System* is when a challenge to an agency action must be filed in court in order to be timely.[26] The Administrative Procedure Act imposes a six-year statute of limitations under Section 2401(a).[27] But is that calculated from the time the agency acts, or is it determined from the time a person is injured by the agency action? The Court, in a 6–3 decision with the majority opinion written by Justice Amy Coney Barrett, chose the latter. Justice Ketanji Brown Jackson wrote a vehement dissent.

The Court began by quoting the relevant language from the statute of limitations: "[E]very civil action commenced against the United States shall be barred unless the complaint is filed within six years after the right of action first accrues."[28] The Court then focused on Section 702 of the Administrative Procedure Act, which entitles a person to judicial review when they are "suffering legal wrong because of agency action, or adversely affected or aggrieved by agency action."[29] The Court concluded that a cause of action accrues when a person is injured. Justice Barrett wrote for the Court: "Section 2401(a) embodies the plaintiff-centric traditional rule that a statute of limitations begins to run only when the plaintiff has a complete and present cause of action. Because injury, not just finality, is required to sue under the APA, Corner Post's cause of action was not complete and present until it was injured."[30]

Justice Jackson, in her dissent, said that the implications of the Court's decision would be "staggering."[31] She disagreed with the majority as to the meaning of "accrues" and expressed great concern that those challenging agency actions could do so indefinitely into the future. She wrote: "This means that, from this day forward, administrative agencies can be sued in perpetuity over every final decision they make."[32] She said that the majority's approach "creates uncertainty for the Government and every entity that relies on the Government to function."[33]

She powerfully concluded her dissent by tying it to the other cases of the term:

> At the end of a momentous Term, this much is clear: The tsunami of lawsuits against agencies that the Court's holdings in this case and *Loper Bright* have authorized has the potential to devastate the functioning of the Federal Government. Even more to the present point, that result simply cannot be what Congress intended when it enacted legislation that stood up and funded federal agencies and vested them with authority to set the ground rules for the individuals and entities that participate in the our [*sic*] economy and our society. It is utterly inconceivable that §2401(a)'s statute of limitations was meant to permit fresh attacks on settled regulations from all new comers forever. Yet, that is what the majority holds today.[34]

Funding of Federal Agencies

There was one important decision that ruled in favor of a federal agency: *Consumer Financial Protection Bureau v. Consumer Financial Services Association of America*.[35] Congress provided an unusual funding mechanism for the Consumer Financial Protection Bureau (CFPB), which is outside the ordinary annual appropriations process. Congress authorized the CFPB to draw from the Federal Reserve System an amount that its director deems "reasonably necessary to carry out" the CFPB's duties, subject only to an inflation-adjusted cap.[36]

The CFPB adopted regulations of high-interest consumer loans in what came to be called "payday lending rules." A challenge was brought, and the U.S. Court of Appeals for the Fifth Circuit held that the funding mechanism for the CFPB was unconstitutional, and therefore effectively everything it has done is unconstitutional, because the funding of the agency did not involve an annual appropriation from Congress.

The Supreme Court, in a 7–2 decision with the majority opinion written by Justice Clarence Thomas, reversed the Fifth Circuit and upheld the funding mechanism for the CFPB. The Court concluded, "Under the Appropriations Clause, an appropriation is simply a law that authorizes expenditures from a specified source of public money for designated purposes. The statute that provides the Bureau's funding meets these requirements. We therefore conclude that the Bureau's funding mechanism does not violate the Appropriations Clause."[37]

The Court stressed that the text of the Constitution was met because Congress had specifically authorized this funding mechanism. The Court also said that this was consistent with history, including ways in which the first Congress funded the customs service and the postal office. After reviewing this history, the Court said: "We conclude that the statute that authorizes the Bureau to draw funds from the combined earnings of the Federal Reserve System is an 'Appropriatio[n] made by Law.' We therefore hold that the requirements of the Appropriations Clause are satisfied."[38]

Justice Alito dissented, joined by Justice Gorsuch.[39] He argued that the Constitution requires an annual appropriation from Congress for a federal agency. He complained that the majority's decision "turns the Appropriations Clause into a minor vestige."[40]

The case is most significant for what it did not do: it did not declare a federal agency unconstitutional, and it did not prevent Congress from creating funding mechanisms without annual appropriations from Congress. In a term when the Court imposed significant limits on administrative power, this case is notable for not doing so.

Conclusion

It is important to look at these three cases that limited administrative agencies together and along with the decisions of the last few years. All of the rulings have strengthened the ability of courts to overturn administrative agency actions. The 6–3 split in each of these cases reflects a deep disagreement over agencies and their role in the American system of government. These decisions individually and cumulatively will have a dramatic impact on federal agencies, federal courts, and society. They also are likely not the last word from the Roberts Court about limiting the power of federal agencies.

Endnotes

1. West Virginia v. EPA, 597 U.S. 697 (2022).
2. Biden v. Nebraska, 600 U.S. 477 (2023).
3. Loper Bright Enters. v. Raimondo, 144 S. Ct. 2244 (2024).
4. Sec. & Exch. Comm'n v. Jarkesy, 144 S. Ct. 2117 (2024).
5. Corner Post, Inc. v. Bd. of Governors of the Fed. Rsrv. Sys., 144 S. Ct. 2440 (2024).
6. Chevron U.S.A. Inc. v. Nat. Res. Def. Council, Inc., 467 U.S. 837 (1984).
7. Loper Bright Enters. v. Raimondo, 458 U.S. App. D.C. 600 (2022); Loper Bright Enters. v. Raimondo, 544 F. Supp. 3d 82 (D.D.C. 2021); Relentless, Inc. v. United States DOC, 62 F.4th 621 (1st Cir. 2023); Relentless Inc. v. United States DOC, 561 F. Supp. 3d 226 (D.R.I. 2021).
8. *Loper Bright Enters.*, 144 S. Ct. at 2265.
9. *Id.* at 2271 (citing Marbury v. Madison, 5 U.S. 137 (1803)).
10. *Id.* at 2261.
11. *Id.* at 2266.
12. *Id.* at 2273.
13. *Id.* at 2311 (Kagan, J., dissenting).
14. *Id.* at 2294.
15. *Id.*
16. *Id.* at 2311.
17. Sec. & Exch. Comm'n v. Jarkesy, 144 S. Ct. 2117, 2139 (2024).
18. *Id.* at 2155 (Sotomayor, J., dissenting).
19. *Id.* at 2127.
20. Erwin Chemerinsky, Federal Jurisdiction 261 (8th ed. 2021).
21. *Jarkesy*, 144 S. Ct. at 2131.
22. *Id.* at 2139.
23. *Id.* at 2155 (Sotomayor, J., dissenting).
24. *Id.* at 2175.
25. *See* Chemerinsky, *supra* note 20, at 261–63.
26. Corner Post, Inc. v. Bd. of Governors of the Fed. Rsrv. Sys., 144 S. Ct. 2440, 2448 (2024).

27. 28 U.S.C. § 2401(a).
28. *Id.*
29. 5 U.S.C. § 702.
30. *Corner Post, Inc.*, 144 S. Ct. at 2452–53.
31. *Id.* at 2470 (Jackson, J., dissenting).
32. *Id.* at 2480.
33. *Id.*
34. *Id.* at 2482.
35. Consumer Fin. Prot. Bureau v. Consumer Fin. Servs. Ass'n of Am., 144 S. Ct. 1474 (2024).
36. 12 U.S.C. § 5497(a)(1), (2).
37. *Consumer Fin. Prot. Bureau*, 144 S. Ct. at 1480.
38. *Id.* at 1486.
39. *Id.* at 1493 (Alito, J., dissenting).
40. *Id.*

4

Bankruptcy Law

Without a doubt, the most important bankruptcy case of the term was *Harrington v. Purdue Pharma L.P.*[1] It is a case of great significance with regard to the opioid crisis in the United States. It also will have important implications for the ability of bankruptcy courts to fashion orders in mass tort cases in the future.

Opioids have been a public health tragedy. It is estimated that 247,000 people in the United States have died from prescription-opioid overdoses.[2] Opioid-involved overdose deaths rose from 49,860 in 2019 to 81,806 in 2022.[3] As the Court noted, the Sackler family–owned Purdue Pharma, which made OxyContin (the trade name for oxycodone), "sits at the center of these events."[4] It is estimated that between 1996 and 2019, Purdue Pharma generated approximately $34 billion in revenue, most of which came from OxyContin sales.

It is estimated that the Sackler family took $11 billion in profits out of the company. In 2019, Purdue Pharma filed for Chapter 11 bankruptcy. The Sacklers proposed a plan where they would pay up to $4.35 billion into a fund that would be used to compensate victims of opioids and for prevention and treatment programs. In exchange, the Sacklers would be completely immune from civil liability, which was an enormous benefit because of the huge number of pending and likely future claims against them. As the Supreme Court explained, "[T]he Sacklers wanted to extinguish any claims the estate might have against family members, including for fraudulently transferring funds from Purdue in the years preceding its bankruptcy. Second, the Sacklers wanted to end the growing number of lawsuits against them brought by opioid victims (the Sackler discharge)."[5]

The bankruptcy court approved the settlement, saying it was a "bitter" result, but approved the plan nonetheless because of the great public benefit that would come from the fund.[6] The federal district court, though, reversed, concluding that the bankruptcy court lacked authority to extinguish claims against the Sacklers without the consent of the opioid victims who brought them.[7]

While the Sacklers appealed to the U.S. Court of Appeals for the Second Circuit, they reached a settlement with the states that had opposed approval of the plan. The Sacklers agreed to contribute an additional $1.175 to $1.675 billion, bringing their total for the fund up to about $6 billion.

The Second Circuit reversed the district court and ruled in favor of the bankruptcy court's authority to approve the plan creating the fund and protecting the Sacklers from future liability.[8]

The Supreme Court, in a 5–4 decision, reversed the Second Circuit and invalidated the plan. There was an unusual lineup of the justices. Justice Neil Gorsuch wrote the opinion for the Court, joined by Justices Thomas, Alito, Barrett, and Jackson. Justice Brett Kavanaugh's dissent was joined by Chief Justice Roberts, who rarely dissents, and liberal Justices Sotomayor and Kagan.

Justice Gorsuch's majority opinion stressed that the bankruptcy court had no authority to give relief to the Sacklers, who were not part of the bankruptcy proceedings, and had no authority to preclude the claims of those who would get no relief.

The Court emphasized that the corporation, Purdue Pharma, had filed for bankruptcy, not the Sacklers. The question, the Court said, was one of interpreting a provision of the Bankruptcy Code, Section 1123(b), that says a bankruptcy plan can "(6) include any other appropriate provision not inconsistent with the applicable provisions of this title."[9] The Court argued that this "catchall" provision had to be interpreted together with the rest of the statute and declared: "[W]e do not think paragraph (6) affords a bankruptcy court the authority the plan proponents suppose."[10] The Court concluded that the issue was not to be resolved by policy considerations, but by statutory interpretation.

The Court stressed what it was not deciding: "As important as the question we decide today are ones we do not. Nothing in what we have said should be construed to call into question *consensual* third-party releases offered in connection with a bankruptcy reorganization plan; those sorts of releases pose different questions and may rest on different legal grounds than the nonconsensual release at issue here."[11] The Court's holding was thus that a bankruptcy court could not approve a plan that provided nondebtors, the Sacklers, relief without the consent of creditors, those with claims against them.

Justice Kavanaugh wrote a strong dissent. He began: "Today's decision is wrong on the law and devastating for more than 100,000 opioid victims and their families. The Court's decision rewrites the text of the U.S. Bankruptcy Code and restricts the long-established authority of bankruptcy courts to fashion fair and equitable relief for mass-tort victims. As a result, opioid victims are now deprived of the substantial monetary recovery that they long fought for and finally secured after years of litigation."[12] He described the plan as "a shining example of the bankruptcy system at work."[13]

He argued that Section 1123(b)(6) of the federal Bankruptcy Code broadly authorizes bankruptcy courts to include "appropriate" relief in their orders so long as they are "not inconsistent with the applicable provisions of" the Bankruptcy Code.[14] He stressed that the Purdue bankruptcy plan has provided compensation to over 100,000 victims of the opioid crisis and significant funding for thousands of state and local governments to prevent and treat opioid addiction. For this reason, the settlement was supported by all 50 state attorneys general, a consensus rarely seen on any issue.

The dissent also raised serious concerns over the ability of bankruptcy courts to provide relief in mass tort cases in the future. Justice Kavanaugh wrote that settlements like this "have enabled substantial and equitable relief to victims in cases ranging from asbestos, Dalkon Shield, and

Dow Corning silicone breast implants to the Catholic Church and the Boy Scouts."[15] Simply put, he said it will be far more difficult to settle mass tort cases—instances where corporate practices have injured a large number of people—without being able to give relief against those who are not parties in the bankruptcy court proceeding. Justice Kavanaugh explained: "The Court's decision deprives the bankruptcy system of a longstanding and critical tool that has been used repeatedly to ensure fair and sizable recovery for victims—to repeat, recovery for *victims*—in mass torts ranging from Dalkon Shield to the Boy Scouts."[16]

The decision was about how to interpret the statutory language of the Bankruptcy Code. The majority chose to read the power of the bankruptcy court to approve a plan with any "appropriate" provision narrowly, while the dissenters wanted to interpret it broadly. But as so often is the case with regard to statutory language, the text does not provide an answer, and each interpretation is reasonable.

For the majority—and perhaps this explains why Justice Jackson was in the majority—there was concern about the fairness of the plan. Although the settlement could cost the Sacklers up to $6 billion, it left them with over $5 billion in profits from OxyContin and completely protected them from all civil liability in the future. The settlement would leave many victims of the opioid crisis with no redress.

But for the dissent it was better to take the $6 billion for all the good that it could provide than accept the uncertainty and cost of countless separate lawsuits. And the dissent thought it important to keep open this tool for settlement in other cases where large numbers of people are hurt by corporate abuses.

Thus, in the end, it is a case of great significance for the opioid crisis: victims and state governments will not receive the promised $6 billion in funds from the Sacklers under the proposed plan and must wait even longer for prevention and treatment funding. It also is a decision of great importance for the power of bankruptcy courts to deal with mass torts in the future. The Court's narrow interpretation of a broad provision, in itself, is likely to have significance beyond this case.

Endnotes

1. Harrington v. Purdue Pharma L.P., 144 S. Ct. 2071 (2024).
2. *Id.* at 2078.
3. Nat'l Inst. on Drug Abuse, *Drug Overdose Death Rates*, NAT'L INSTS. OF HEALTH (May 14, 2024), https://nida.nih.gov/research-topics/trends-statistics/overdose-death-rates.
4. *Harrington*, 144 S. Ct. at 2078.
5. *Id.* at 2079 (citations omitted).
6. *In re* Purdue Pharma L.P., 633 B.R. 53, 101 (Bankr. S.D.N.Y. 2021).
7. *In re* Purdue Pharma, L.P., 635 B.R. 26, 89, 115 (S.D.N.Y. 2021).
8. Purdue Pharma, L.P. v. City of Grande Prairie (*In re* Pharma L.P.), 69 F.4th 45, 57 (2d Cir. 2023).
9. 11 U.S.C. § 1123(b)(6).
10. *Harrington*, 144 S. Ct. at 2083 (2024).
11. *Id.* at 2087.
12. *Id.* at 2088 (Kavanaugh, J., dissenting).
13. *Id.*
14. *Id.* at 2091.
15. *Id.* at 2089.
16. *Id.* at 2104.

5

Business and Tax Law Cases

As always, there were several cases involving business and tax law. The highest-profile case, *Moore v. United States*, involved the 16th Amendment and had the potential to upend many aspects of the tax system.[1] But the Court upheld the tax and thus the case is most significant for what the Court did not do. There also were two narrow decisions about arbitration and a case about copyright law.

Federal Taxes

In *Moore v. United States*, the Supreme Court considered a provision under the 2017 Tax Cuts and Jobs Act known as the Mandatory Repatriation Tax (MRT) and upheld it as constitutional under Sections 8 and 9 of Article I and the 16th Amendment.[2] The MRT imposed a "new, one-time pass-through tax on some American shareholders of American-controlled foreign corporations."[3] The MRT aimed to strengthen "subpart F," a pass-through tax enacted in 1962, which "attributes certain income, mostly passive income, of American-controlled foreign corporations to their American shareholders and then taxes those shareholders on that income."[4] Under the MRT, American shareholders were required to pay a retroactive tax on additional parts of a foreign business's income that had not yet been taxed in the United States, even though these gains had not been realized by the shareholders through any dividends. Both subpart F and the MRT aim to prevent people from evading tax liability by moving their income into foreign corporations that cannot be taxed by the United States.

The plaintiffs in *Moore* were Charles and Kathleen Moore, who maintained a 13-percent ownership share in an American-controlled corporation based in India, KisanKraft.[5] The corporation generated significant income supplying power tools to Indian farmers between 2006 and 2017, yet "neither KisanKraft nor the Moores had paid U.S. taxes on that income" because "KisanKraft had not distributed that income to its American shareholders."[6] Under the MRT, the Moores were required to pay $14,729 in taxes for KisanKraft's profits over 11 years that had neither been taxed by the U.S. government nor been distributed to the shareholders.

They sued in the Western District of Washington for a refund. On appeal their argument was that the MRT violated the Direct Tax Clause of the Constitution because the MRT was an unapportioned direct tax on their shares of KisanKraft stock. The Court upheld the tax as a permissible exercise of Congress's taxing power.[7] Justice Kavanaugh wrote the majority opinion, which was joined by Chief Justice Roberts and Justices Kagan, Sotomayor, and Jackson. Justice Jackson wrote a concurrence. Justice Barrett also wrote a concurrence, joined by Justice Alito. Justice Thomas wrote a dissent joined by Justice Gorsuch.

Both the District Court and the Ninth Circuit ruled the MRT to be a lawful indirect income tax because "KisanKraft earned significant income, and the MRT assigns only a pro-rata share of that income to the Moores."[8] The Supreme Court upheld these decisions, determining that the MRT is not a direct tax on the property of shareholders but is instead an indirect tax on the income of a foreign corporation that had not yet paid taxes in the United States. The Court declared: "[T]he precise and narrow question that the Court addresses today is whether Congress may attribute an entity's realized and undistributed income to the entity's shareholders or partners, and then tax the shareholders or partners on their portions of that income. This Court's longstanding precedents, reflected in and reinforced by Congress's longstanding practice, establish that the answer is yes."[9]

Justice Kavanaugh concluded that the MRT is constitutional because it "operates in the same basic way as Congress's longstanding taxation of partnerships, S corporations,[10] and subpart F income" because it "attributes the undistributed income of American-controlled foreign corporations to their American shareholders, and then taxes the American shareholders on that income."[11] Congress may opt to "tax a business entity itself on the income that the entity earns" or "treat an entity as a pass-through—attributing the entity's undistributed income to the shareholders or partners and then taxing the shareholders or partners on that income. Either way, this Court has held that the tax remains a tax on income—and thus an indirect tax that need not be apportioned."[12]

The majority began explaining its reasoning by outlining the broad principles underlying Congress's expansive taxation power. Congress tends to impose indirect taxes on activities and transactions that must "be uniform throughout the United States" rather than direct taxes that require apportionment among the states.[13] Income taxes have been repeatedly upheld as indirect taxes that do not require apportionment, as confirmed by the 16th Amendment.[14]

The Moores argued that the MRT was a direct tax on property rather than an indirect tax on income because they had not realized any gains from their investment in KisanKraft, which had not distributed any profits to the shareholders. However, the majority determined that "the MRT *does* tax realized income—namely, income realized by the corporation, KisanKraft. The MRT attributes the income of the corporation to the shareholders, and then taxes the shareholders (including the Moores) on their share of that undistributed corporate income."[15]

Next, the majority cited a series of cases upholding the constitutionality of pass-through taxes. Established by Congress in 1962, subpart F "treats certain foreign corporations as pass-throughs by attributing undistributed income of foreign corporations to their American shareholders, and then taxing the American shareholders on their pro rata shares of the income."[16] Federal courts of appeals have repeatedly upheld that law.[17] The majority concluded that subpart F and the MRT are similar enough that if the former is constitutional, the latter is as well.

In terms of public policy, Justice Kavanaugh noted that the plaintiffs' argument that "a tax attributing an entity's undistributed income to its shareholders or partners is not an income tax" would mean that "all of those taxes are unconstitutional and that all of those precedents should be overruled."[18] Later on he noted that "the Moores' argument, taken to its logical conclusion, could render vast swaths of the Internal Revenue Code unconstitutional."[19] Eliminating those tax provisions "would deprive the U.S. Government and the American people of trillions in lost tax revenue," requiring either spending cuts or significant tax hikes.[20] That is why the case is most significant for what the Court didn't do.

Justice Jackson joined the majority in full. In her concurrence, she emphasized the Constitution's grant of "plenary power" over taxation to Congress.[21] She noted that the plaintiffs would have faced additional hurdles should they have prevailed on the narrow question of whether the MRT is a direct or indirect tax. First, the Court would "need to agree with petitioners that Congress can tax income only if it is actually received or 'realized,'" a requirement that is not supported by the 16th Amendment, precedent, or historical understandings of the term "income."[22] Second, the Court would "need to confirm that the tax was a direct tax before requiring apportionment."[23] The MRT may also be a lawful indirect tax on Americans that does not require apportionment if construed as "an excise tax on the privilege of doing business through a controlled foreign corporation."[24]

She concluded that the Court should take a restrained approach when considering the policy outcomes of tax policy and should instead leave those issues to voters and the legislative branch.

Justice Barrett, joined by Justice Alito, concurred in the judgment, but she disagreed with significant portions of the majority's reasoning.[25] She is far more skeptical of Congress's ability to tax businesses through pass-through mechanisms, yet she concurs in judgment based on the specifics of the MRT and the oral arguments. Justice Barrett said that "precedent does not give Congress carte blanche to attribute corporate income to a shareholder. Instead, it suggests that Congress has a limited power to do so that depends on the relationship between the shareholder and the income."[26] She said "that the Court today is too quick to bless the attribution of corporate income to shareholders."[27] She emphasized that "the Constitution prohibits Congress from arbitrarily attributing to the taxpayer someone else's income."[28] However, Justice Barrett acknowledged that the government provided a reasonably nonarbitrary framework to tax foreign companies that are otherwise "outside the reach of an accumulated earnings tax."[29]

From the beginning of the concurrence, Justice Barrett reframed the case: "The question on which we granted review is '[w]hether the Sixteenth Amendment authorizes Congress to tax unrealized sums without apportionment among the states.' The answer is straightforward: No."[30]

Justice Barrett distinguished "property" and "income" from one another: property is the "seed" and income is the "fruit that it will yield."[31] Therefore, she argued that "[t]he Sixteenth Amendment's reference to income 'derived' from any source encompasses a requirement that income, to be taxed without apportionment, must be *realized*."[32] She posited that "realize" and "derive" are essentially synonyms based on common understandings of the terms when the 16th Amendment was ratified and based on prior court precedents.

She then concluded that "the Moores have not realized income from their KisanKraft shares" because the corporation has yet to distribute profits to shareholders.[33] She rejected the notion that Congress may impose "an unapportioned tax on appreciation" and argued that the Court has only looked to asset appreciation when determining "how much of the corporation's *income* could be taxed under the statute" instead of treating "asset appreciation itself . . . as taxable as income."[34] Therefore, she concluded that "precedent uniformly holds that [realization] is required before the Government may tax financial gain without apportionment."[35]

However, she recognized that while "the Moores did not realize income as shareholders, KisanKraft realized income as a corporation."[36] She then asked: "[C]an Congress disregard KisanKraft's corporate form, attribute KisanKraft's income to its shareholders, and tax its shareholders on that income?"[37]

She disagreed with the majority that Congress "can treat corporations interchangeably with partnerships, whose partners have always been subject to pass-through taxation."[38] Instead, she found that Congress may "disregard the corporate form to determine whether the shareholder received income *in substance*, if not in form."[39] She argues that Congress must pay special attention to "matters of corporate form" and that Congress only has "a limited power" to tax the shareholders of a company rather than the company itself.[40]

Justice Thomas wrote a dissent joined by Justice Gorsuch. He found that "[b]ecause the Moores never actually received any of their investment gains, those unrealized gains could not be taxed as 'income' under the Sixteenth Amendment."[41] He asserted that realization of income is a requirement for taxation and that the majority improperly focused on whether "Congress can attribute the undistributed income of an entity to the entity's shareholders or partners."[42]

Focusing on the history and text of the 16th Amendment, Justice Thomas concluded that "income" "refers only to income realized by the taxpayer."[43] He analyzed "disputes over the scope of the Direct Tax Clause between the founding and the expiration of the Civil War income tax," failed constitutional challenges against the Civil War income tax, and the 1895 case *Pollock v. Farmers' Loan & Trust Co.* that struck down an income tax by finding it to be a direct tax that had not been properly apportioned among the states.[44]

He noted that "[t]he Sixteenth Amendment was designed to overrule *Pollock*'s obstacle to an income tax, and it was understood by the public in those terms."[45] However, he found the text of the 16th Amendment to narrowly "abolish *Pollock*'s rule that an income tax is a direct tax if a tax on the source of the income would be a direct tax."[46] He also argued that "the Sixteenth Amendment left everything else in place, including the federalism principles bound up in the division between direct and indirect taxes."[47]

He drew two conclusions from the history leading up to the 16th Amendment: "First, because the Amendment abolished *Pollock*'s rule that an income tax must be classified as direct or indirect based on whether a tax on the *source* of that income would be direct or indirect, the Amendment created a constitutional distinction between income and its source. Second, because Sixteenth Amendment 'income' must be distinguished from its source, the Amendment includes a realization requirement."[48]

He analyzed the text of the amendment and dictionaries from the time of its ratification to find that the federal government may properly leverage indirect taxes on "income," yet it cannot tax the "source" from which that income is "derived" without apportionment among the states.[49] Therefore, Congress may only impose an indirect tax on "income," defined as realized gains, and cannot impose an indirect tax on the "source" from which income is derived or realized, which is a form of property. He found that a tax on both the income and the source of that income "whether it be an increase in assets, unsold property, or securities, would be a tax on the value of real estate or property, and should therefore require apportionment under the Direct Tax Clause."[50]

He then went on to criticize the attribution doctrine established by the majority, which focused on whether a foreign company's income can be attributed to the shareholders. He disagreed with the majority's characterization of a variety of cases and concluded that "none of the cases supports the proposition that the Sixteenth Amendment empowers Congress to freely attribute income to any taxpayer it reasonably chooses."[51]

The case is most significant for what it did not decide. Justice Kavanaugh repeatedly emphasized the narrowness of the ruling: "It is limited to: (i) taxation of the shareholders of an entity, (ii) on the undistributed income realized by the entity, (iii) which has been attributed to the shareholders, (iv) when the entity itself has not been taxed on that income. In other words, our holding applies when Congress treats the entity as a pass-through."[52]

The case notably did not address the question of whether Congress may or may not tax unrealized gains. Although "the Moores argue that realization is a constitutional requirement" and "the Government argues that it is not," the Court did not "resolve that disagreement over realization."[53] Both "the dissent and the opinion concurring in the judgment focus primarily on the realization issue—namely, whether realization is required for an income tax," but the majority did not find it necessary to resolve that question in this case because they found that KisanKraft had realized profits that had not yet been taxed.[54] Therefore, the Court narrowly held that if an American-owned foreign corporation has realized profits without distributing them and has not paid American taxes on those gains, Congress may lawfully impose a pass-through tax that requires the American shareholders to pay the tax on that corporate income.

As explained earlier, the majority's decision affirming the legitimacy of pass-through taxes avoided a potentially catastrophic outcome. Justices Thomas and Gorsuch wanted to rule that all taxes on unrealized gains are inherently unconstitutional under the 16th Amendment, meaning that pass-through taxes could no longer be upheld as a constitutional form of income taxation. Their interpretation would have affected other areas of the tax code and made it even easier for the extremely wealthy to hide their money in offshore tax havens and domestic shell companies.

The Tax Foundation put together an analysis showing that if "the Supreme Court [struck] down taxes on all undistributed business earnings," it would "eliminat[e] the taxation of pass-through and corporate retained earnings [and] would reduce federal revenue by nearly $5.7 trillion over 10 years."[55] A broad prohibition on pass-through taxes would also make it next to impossible for the United States to comply with efforts to establish a 15 percent Global Corporation Minimum Tax, as American billionaires could easily shield themselves from income tax liability by hiding their assets in foreign corporations on which they do not need to pay U.S. taxes.[56]

While commentators feared the Supreme Court would preemptively rule a potential wealth tax to be unconstitutional,[57] Justice Kavanaugh made clear that "our analysis today does not address the distinct issues that would be raised by (i) an attempt by Congress to tax both the entity and the shareholders or partners on the entity's undistributed income; (ii) taxes on holdings, wealth, or net worth; or (iii) taxes on appreciation."[58]

Despite the opinion's not explicitly addressing the wealth tax issue, commentators have expressed concerns that "Kavanaugh's *Moore* opinion includes a bonanza of loaded language that any competent tax lawyer can seize upon to protect their richest clients from wealth taxes."[59]

According to Ian Millhiser at Vox, the majority's declaration that "direct taxes are those taxes imposed on persons or property" (instead of indirect taxes on income) would likely require a wealth tax to be apportioned among the states in an administrative nightmare.[60] We will not know the constitutional legitimacy of a wealth tax until Congress imposes one, which does not seem likely to happen any time soon.

Copyright Law

The issue in *Warner Chappell Music, Inc. v. Nealy* was how to calculate the period of damages for a copyright violation.[61] In a 6–3 decision, the Court held that any plaintiff with a timely claim under the Copyright Act's statute of limitation "can get damages going back more than three years" because "[t]he Copyright Act contains no separate time-based limit on monetary recovery."[62]

Sherman Nealy and Tony Butler formed Music Specialist, Inc. in 1983 and "released one album and several singles."[63] Nealy was imprisoned for drug-related offenses from 1989 to 2008 and from 2012 to 2015.[64] While Nealy was in prison, Butler "entered into an agreement with Warner Chappell Music, Inc. to license works from the Music Specialist catalog."[65] The artist Flo Rida used portions of music originally released by Music Specialist and released the song "In the Ayer" that "sold millions of copies and reached No. 9 on the Billboard chart," while other Music Specialist songs "found their way into recordings by the Black Eyed Peas and Kid Sister."[66] Nealy sued Warner Chappell in 2018 for copyright infringement, arguing that the company had infringed his rights as early as 2008, ten years before Nealy sued.[67]

The Copyright Act contains a provision requiring the plaintiff to file suit "within three years after the claim accrued."[68] Based on precedent in the 11th Circuit, both parties rejected the notion that a claim accrues when "an infringing act occurs" and instead accepted the "discovery rule" that provides "a claim accrues when 'the plaintiff discovers, or with due diligence should have discovered,' the infringing act."[69] The key question thus became damages calculations.

The district court found "that even if Nealy could sue under that rule for infringements going back ten years, he could recover damages or profits for only those occurring in the last three."[70] The 11th Circuit reversed and ruled that "a plaintiff with a timely claim under the discovery rule may obtain 'retrospective relief for [an] infringement' even if it 'occurr[ed] more than three years before the lawsuit's filing.'"[71]

Justice Kagan delivered the majority opinion. Justices Gorsuch, Thomas, and Alito dissented. The Supreme Court affirmed the 11th Circuit's decision, resolving a circuit split, and held that any plaintiff with a timely claim under the Copyright Act's statute of limitation can get damages going back more than three years. In this case, Nealy was allowed to recover ten years of damages going back to the initial infringement and was not limited to three years of damages going back to when he discovered the infringement.

The Court "assume[d] without deciding that a claim is timely under that provision if brought within three years of when the plaintiff discovered an infringement, no matter when the infringement happened."[72] The Court made this assumption because the parties had previously agreed to the "discovery rule" that "a copyright claim accrues when a plaintiff discovers or should have discovered an infringement, rather than when the infringement happened."[73] Justice Kagan's decision flowed logically from that assumption; the Copyright Act does not specify a "time limit on monetary recovery. So a copyright owner possessing a timely claim for infringement is entitled to damages, no matter when the infringement occurred."[74]

Justice Gorsuch dissented, joined by Justices Thomas and Alito, and strongly criticized the discovery rule and its application to the Copyright Act. He argued that "the Act almost certainly does not tolerate a discovery rule," so "rather than devote our time to this case, I would have dismissed it as improvidently granted and awaited another squarely presenting the question whether the Copyright Act authorizes the discovery rule. Better, in my view, to answer a question that does matter than one that almost certainly does not."[75] He argued that the discovery rule should only apply "in cases of fraud or concealment" absent clear direction by Congress, "consistent with traditional equitable practice" because the Court has warned "against taking any more 'expansive approach to the discovery rule.'"[76]

Going forward, there is uncertainty about when a copyright infringement claim "accrues" and when a plaintiff may file suit; are lower courts to use the incident of injury rule or the discovery rule? The Supreme Court intentionally chose to not address that question. Although Justice Gorsuch called to reconsider the application of the discovery rule to the Copyright Act, the Supreme Court denied a petition for a writ of certiorari on that exact question on May 20, 2024.[77]

The ruling in *Warner Chappell* may help plaintiffs in copyright disputes going forward. Should plaintiffs successfully file an infringement claim, they will not face a time limit on how much they can recover in damages. However, it is uncertain how often the discovery rule will permit copyright infringement claims that would not be permitted under the incident of injury rule. The discovery rule still looks to when the plaintiff "with due diligence should have discovered" the copyright infringement.

Nealy's fact pattern was unique; he could not reasonably have been expected to learn of the infringement when he was in prison and his business partner signed away the rights without informing him. However, for most artists, they or their record studio likely is expected to promptly discover an infringement of their copyright, especially if that infringement helps produce a hit song.

Arbitration

The Supreme Court decided two narrow cases regarding the Federal Arbitration Act (FAA). Both *Coinbase v. Suski* and *Bissonnette v. LePage Bakeries Park St., LLC* were decided by 9–0 margins in favor of the parties attempting to avoid forced arbitration. Both cases were remanded, so there is still a possibility that the respective circuit courts will rule to compel arbitration.

In *Coinbase*, users of the cryptocurrency platform entered two contracts that conflicted on whether their claims against Coinbase would be adjudicated in front of an arbitrator or a court. The Court held that a judge and not an arbitrator must decide which contract governs and which issues are arbitrable by the arbitrator.

In *Bissonnette*, the Court considered who qualifies as a "transportation worker" that is exempt from forced arbitration requirements in the FAA. The Court decided that a person can be a transportation worker without working for a transportation company.

These decisions are somewhat notable given that "the court in the last few decades has heard numerous cases under the FAA. . . . And in almost all of those cases the justices, often by closely divided votes, have accepted the arguments of businesses to force [workers] into arbitration."[78]

However, both decisions were very narrow and based on straightforward application of law, so they are unlikely to have major impacts on arbitration law going forward. In fact, Columbia Law Professor Ronald Mann said, "My strong sense is that [Coinbase] turned out to be a minor and unusual dispute that the justices wish they had left alone."[79]

Endnotes

1. Moore v. United States, 144 S. Ct. 1680 (2024).
2. *Id.*
3. *Id.* at 1686.
4. *Id.* at 1685.
5. *Id.* at 1686.
6. *Id.*
7. *Id.* at 1688.
8. *Id.* at 1686 (citing Moore v. United States, 36 F.4th 930, 936–37 (2022)).
9. *Id.* at 1688–89.
10. *Id.* at 1685 ("S corporations are corporations with 100 or fewer shareholders where the shareholders have elected to be taxed on a pass-through basis.").
11. *Id.* at 1696.
12. *Id.* at 1689.
13. *Id.* at 1687.
14. *Id.* at 1688.
15. *Id.*
16. *Id.* at 1690.
17. *Id.*

18. *Id.* at 1691–93.

19. *Id.* at 1696 ("See, *e.g.*, 26 U. S. C. §305(c) (deemed stock distributions); §§446, 448 (accrual accounting); §701 (partnership taxation); §§951–965 (subpart F); §951A (pass-through tax on global intangible low-taxed income); §1256(a) (certain futures contracts); §1272(a) (original-issue discount instruments); §§1361–1379 (S corporations); §§2501–2524 (gift taxes).").

20. *Id.*

21. *Id.* at 1697 (Jackson, J., concurring).

22. *Id.* at 1698.

23. *Id.* at 1699.

24. *Id.*

25. *Id.* at 1700 (Barrett, J., concurring).

26. *Id.* at 1707.

27. *Id.* at 1708.

28. *Id.*

29. *Id.* ("One is whether the taxpayer has 'sufficient power and control over . . . the income' that it is 'reasonable to treat him as the recipient of the income for tax purposes.' *Commissioner v. Sunnen*, 333 U. S. 591, 604 (1948). Another is whether the taxpayer receives a special 'privilege or benefit' from the entity that earns the income. *Burnet*, 289 U. S., at 679. A third is whether the corporation is foreign and thus outside the reach of an accumulated earnings tax. Cf. *Ivan Allen Co.*, 422 U. S., at 624. These factors may serve as a useful guide for lower courts when applying today's decision to taxes that attribute income from other types of corporations to an individual taxpayer.").

30. *Id.* at 1700.

31. *Id.* at 1701.

32. *Id.*

33. *Id.* at 1702.

34. *Id.* at 1702–03.

35. *Id.* at 1704.

36. *Id.*

37. *Id.*

38. *Id.* at 1705.

39. *Id.*

40. *Id.* at 1707.

41. *Id.* at 1709 (Thomas, J., dissenting).

42. *Id.* at 1710.

43. *Id.*

44. *Id.* at 1717.

45. *Id.* at 1719.

46. *Id.* at 1720.

47. *Id.*; *see id.* at 1718–19 ("[T]he Direct Tax Clause was a federalism provision at the heart of the constitutional compromise: 'If, by calling a tax indirect when it is essentially direct, the rule of protection could be frittered away, one of the great landmarks defining the boundary between the Nation and the States of which it is composed, would have disappeared, and with it one of the bulwarks of private rights and private property.'").

48. *Id.* at 1720.

49. *Id.* at 1722.

50. *Id.*

51. *Id.* at 1723.

52. *Id.* at 1696.

53. *Id.* at 1697.

54. *Id.* at 1696.

55. Daniel Bunn, Alan Cole, William McBride & Garrett Watson, *How the Moore Supreme Court Case Could Reshape Taxation of Unrealized Income*, Tax Found. (Aug. 30, 2023), https://taxfoundation.org/research/all/federal/moore-v-united-states-tax-unrealized-income/.

56. *Id.*

57. Ian Millhiser, *The Supreme Court Case Seeking to Shut Down Wealth Taxes Before They Even Exist*, Vox (Nov. 27, 2023), https://www.vox.com/scotus/2023/11/27/23970859/supreme-court-wealth-tax-moore-united-states.

58. *Moore*, 144 S. Ct. at 1689 n.2.

59. Ian Millhiser, *The Supreme Court's New Tax Decision Is Great News for Billionaires*, Vox (June 20, 2024), https://www.vox.com/scotus/355969/supreme-court-moore-us-wealth-tax-billionaires.

60. *Id.*

61. Warner Chappell Music, Inc. v. Nealy, 144 S. Ct. 1135 (2024).

62. *Id.* at 1139–40.

63. *Id.* at 1137.

64. *Id.*

65. *Id.*

66. *Id.*

67. *Id.*

68. *Id.*

69. *Id.* at 1138.

70. *Id.*

71. *Id.*

72. *Id.* at 1137.

73. *Id.* at 1139.

74. *Id.*

75. *Id.* at 1140–41 (Gorsuch, J., dissenting).

76. *Id.* at 1141.

77. Hearst Newspapers, L.L.C. v. Martinelli, No. 23-474, *cert. denied* (May 20, 2024), https://www.supremecourt.gov/search.aspx?filename=/docket/docketfiles/html/public/23-474.html.

78. Ronald Mann, *Wonder Bread Truck Drivers Seek Exemption from Mandatory Arbitration*, SCOTUSBLOG (Feb. 16, 2024), https://www.scotusblog.com/2024/02/wonder-bread-truck-drivers-seek-exemption-from-mandatory-arbitration/.

79. Ronald Mann, *Courts Rather Than Arbitrators to Decide Whether Dogecoin Dispute Goes to Arbitration*, SCOTUSBLOG (May 28, 2024), https://www.scotusblog.com/2024/05/courts-rather-than-arbitrators-to-decide-whether-dogecoin-dispute-goes-to-arbitration/.

6

Criminal Law and Criminal Procedure

Although the Court's criminal docket did not generate the headlines of the term, the Court decided a number of important cases concerning criminal law and procedure. Interestingly, for the third year in a row, the Court did not decide any cases about the Fourth Amendment and search and seizure, even though there are many fascinating issues dividing the lower courts. The significant criminal law and procedure cases this term involved the Armed Career Criminal Act, the Confrontation Clause, federal criminal statutes, and sentencing.

Armed Career Criminal Act

Erlinger v. United States has the potential for being one of the more important criminal law rulings of the term, with implications beyond the Armed Career Criminal Act (ACCA).[1] In *Apprendi v. New Jersey*, in 2000, the Supreme Court held that any factor, other than a prior conviction, that leads to a sentence greater than the statutory maximum must be proven to the jury beyond a reasonable doubt.[2] The qualification that this principle does not apply to a prior conviction was based on a decision from two years earlier, *Almendarez-Torres v. United States*.[3] There have been countless petitions for certiorari over the last quarter century urging the Court to reconsider *Almendarez-Torres*, but all have been denied. *Erlinger v. United States* rejects the application of *Almendarez-Torres* in the context of the ACCA and raises the possibility that the Court might finally reconsider *Almendarez-Torres*.

The issue in *Erlinger* is whether a defendant facing potential heightened punishment under the ACCA has a Sixth Amendment right to a jury determination of whether his predicate offenses were committed on different occasions. In 2019, Paul Erlinger was charged and pled guilty to unlawful possession of a firearm as a felon under 18 U.S.C. § 922(g), a conviction ordinarily carrying a sentence of up to ten years in prison. The government also charged Erlinger under the ACCA, which imposes a mandatory minimum of 15 years (and a maximum of life) for violations of § 922(g) by defendants found to have had three prior convictions for "violent felonies or serious drug offenses that were committed on occasions different from one another."[4] In pleading guilty, Erlinger acknowledged that although his criminal record contained prior convictions, "his previous convictions were more than a decade old and since then he had turned his life around, secured a steady job, built a family, and remained free from drugs."[5] At sentencing, the judge acknowledged that in light of Erlinger's circumstances, "a 5-year prison term would represent a 'fair sentence,'" but because the judge "found it more likely than not that Mr. Erlinger's past included three ACCA-qualifying offenses committed on three different occasions," the court lacked the authority to issue a five-year sentence due to the ACCA's 15-year mandatory minimum.[6]

Shortly after Erlinger was sentenced, the Seventh Circuit "issued decisions indicating that two of the three offenses on which the district court had relied to invoke ACCA did not qualify as 'violent felonies' or 'serious drug offenses,'" meaning Erlinger no longer had the three prior convictions that the ACCA requires for enhanced punishment.[7] The district court vacated Erlinger's sentence and set a hearing for new sentencing. At sentencing, prosecutors again pushed for enhanced ACCA punishment, this time pointing to "a new set of prior convictions arising from burglaries Mr. Erlinger committed when he was 18 years old—some 26 years before his §922(g) charge."[8] The government argued that "within a span of days," Erlinger had burglarized four establishments and that each burglary "could serve as an ACCA predicate and collectively they could support an ACCA sentence."[9] By contrast, Erlinger argued that "his decades-old burglaries had not occurred on four separate occasions but during a single criminal episode, all of which meant he still lacked the three prior offenses ACCA requires."[10] Erlinger further argued that whether his burglaries constituted a single criminal episode or multiple separate offenses under the ACCA was a factual finding for which he was entitled to a jury under the Fifth and Sixth Amendments. The district court rejected Erlinger's jury argument and found for itself that each burglary constituted a separate offense, again requiring that Erlinger receive the ACCA's mandatory 15-year minimum prison sentence that the district court had no discretion to lessen.[11]

On appeal, Erlinger argued that he was entitled to a jury determination of facts regarding his prior burglaries. The government agreed with Erlinger's position and "confessed error," acknowledging that the Constitution requires a unanimous jury finding beyond reasonable doubt on the issue of whether Erlinger's ACCA predicates were "committed on occasions different from one another."[12]

Nonetheless, the Seventh Circuit affirmed the district court and the sentence.[13] Because the United States confessed error, the Supreme Court granted certiorari and appointed counsel to defend the Seventh Circuit's conclusion. The Supreme Court, in a 6–3 decision, reversed the Seventh Circuit and held that the Fifth and Sixth Amendments guarantee that when a defendant is charged under the ACCA and the number of the defendant's qualifying prior offenses is at issue, the defendant is entitled to a jury determination of those facts. There was an unusual split among the justices. Justice Gorsuch wrote a majority opinion joined by Chief Justice Roberts and Justices Thomas, Sotomayor, Kagan, and Barrett. Justices Kavanaugh, Alito, and Jackson dissented.

The Court began by stressing the importance of jury trials under the Fifth and Sixth Amendments and describing them as fundamental reservations of power to the American people that prevent prosecutorial overreach and misconduct. Justice Gorsuch explained that "only a jury may find facts that increase the prescribed range of penalties to which a criminal defendant is exposed," be it the maximum or the minimum sentence a defendant faces.[14]

Justice Gorsuch noted that sentencing Erlinger under the ACCA according to the facts found by the district court judge would have increased both the minimum and maximum sentence associated with his crime, as instead of him facing zero to ten years in prison, the ACCA would have Erlinger face 15 years to life in prison. Justice Gorsuch thus explained that whether the four burglaries Erlinger committed 26 years ago should be counted as one criminal offense or as at least three distinct offenses is a critical finding of fact that determines whether enhanced sentencing would apply. Thus, it should have been left to a jury to decide.

The Court then addressed whether *Almendarez-Torres* provides an exception to the rule that findings of fact that affect a defendant's sentencing must be left to the jury. But the Court said that *Almendarez-Torres* is considered "as 'at best an exceptional departure' from 'historic practice.'"[15] Justice Gorsuch observed that Justice Thomas, who provided the fifth vote in *Almendarez-Torres*'s 5–4 majority, has since called for it to be overruled. The Court said that no party requested that *Almendarez-Torres* be revisited and that there is no need to do so in this case, as *Almendarez-Torres* "persists as a 'narrow exception' permitting judges to find only 'the fact of a prior conviction'" limited to determining "what crime, with what elements, the defendant was convicted of."[16] Justice Gorsuch explained that the *Almendarez-Torres* exception does not apply because determining whether Erlinger's prior convictions "triggered ACCA's enhanced penalties" required the district court "to do more than identify his previous convictions and the legal elements required to sustain them. It had to find that those offenses occurred on at least three separate occasions."[17]

The Court said that the sentencing court exceeded its bounds in "assum[ing] for itself the responsibility of deciding whether Mr. Erlinger's past offenses differed enough in time, location, character, and purpose to have transpired on different occasions," as those are precisely the sorts of conclusions the Fifth and Sixth Amendments require to be left to the jury.[18] The Court recognized that "in many cases the occasions inquiry will be 'straightforward'" but observed that "none of that means a judge rather than a jury should make the call" due to the rights afforded to defendants under the Fifth and Sixth Amendments.[19]

Finally, the Court addressed the practical issues, such as whether leaving it to a jury to decide whether past convictions constitute a single or multiple offenses might prejudice a defendant since it would allow prosecutors "'to regale juries with the details' of the defendant's past misconduct."[20] Justice Gorsuch explained that "traditional tools exist to address the prejudicial effect evidence about a defendant's past crimes can have on a jury," such as bifurcating proceedings to first have a jury determine whether or not a defendant is guilty and only after returning a guilty verdict have the jury "consider evidence regarding whether the defendant's prior offenses occurred on different occasions for purposes of applying ACCA's mandatory minimum sentence under §924(e)."[21] Bifurcation, Justice Gorsuch explains, is both fair, generally agreed to by both sides in ACCA cases, and something the government has not "been able to anticipate as to why [it] wouldn't agree to."[22]

Justice Thomas wrote a concurring opinion urging that the Court "should revisit *Almendarez-Torres* and correct the 'error to which [he] succumbed' by joining that decision."[23] Justice Thomas said that the time has come to overturn *Almendarez-Torres* once and for all.[24]

There were two dissenting opinions by Justices Kavanaugh and Jackson. Justice Kavanaugh argued that the Supreme Court's precedents "establish that a judge may make the different-occasions determination."[25] He argued that Supreme Court precedent interprets the Sixth Amendment "to draw a clear line between (i) the facts about the present crime that a jury must decide at trial and (ii) the facts about past crimes that a judge may determine at sentencing."[26] Justice Kavanaugh stressed that *Apprendi* did not overrule *Almendarez-Torres* and that he would oppose doing so.[27] He wrote that "overruling *Almendarez-Torres* would upend that settled practice" by forcing legislatures to "choose among various bad options" such as "jettison[ing] longstanding sentencing enhancements for recidivists" or "mandat[ing] costly and inefficient bifurcated trials in cases" where recidivism issues are raised.[28]

Justice Jackson also wrote a dissenting opinion in which she argued that *Apprendi* was "wrongly decided" and objected to extending the

Apprendi rule to recidivist factfinding. Justice Jackson explained that "the Court made a serious mistake when it conflated elements and sentencing factors" in *Apprendi*.[29] She wrote that *Apprendi* has "stunted our collective pursuit of justice."[30] According to Justice Jackson, although the Sixth Amendment "vests juries with sentencing power," the effect of *Apprendi* is to "oust the legislature from its rightful place in the sentencing policy sphere" so "the policymaking branches of our government can no longer devise more nuanced, creative approaches to factfinding at sentencing that better reflect the differing competencies of jurors and judges."[31]

Erlinger is important for defendants charged under the ACCA who have criminal histories where the number of their predicate offenses is unclear. *Erlinger* says that any time there is a question regarding how many predicate offenses a defendant has that might subject them to enhanced ACCA punishment, defendants have the right for that question to be decided by a jury. But the case may have larger significance in suggesting that a majority of the justices are finally willing to overrule *Almendarez-Torres*.

Confrontation Clause

In *Crawford v. Washington* in 2004, the Supreme Court held that it violates the Confrontation Clause of the Sixth Amendment for testimonial statements from an unavailable witness to be admitted against a criminal defendant even if they are reliable.[32] Five years later, the Court applied this in *Melendez-Diaz v. Massachusetts*, finding it to be a violation of the Confrontation Clause for a prosecutor to submit a chemical drug test report without the testimony of the person who performed the test.[33] And in *Bullcoming v. New Mexico*, the Court relied on *Melendez-Diaz* to hold that a State could not introduce one lab analyst's written findings through the testimony of another.[34]

But then in 2012 in *Williams v. Illinois*, the Court created great confusion by deciding without a majority opinion that the Confrontation Clause was not violated by introducing a lab report without the testimony of the technician who performed the test or wrote the report.[35]

The Illinois Supreme Court in that case had ruled that the Confrontation Clause does not apply when testimony is not admitted for the truth of the matter asserted. Although five justices rejected that approach, the absence of a majority opinion engendered great confusion in the lower courts.

Smith v. Arizona helps to resolve some of that confusion.[36] The case had simple facts. In December 2019, Arizona law enforcement officers, while executing a search warrant, found Jason Smith in a shed with what appeared to be various drugs and drug-related items. Smith was charged with possessing dangerous drugs for sale, possessing marijuana for sale, possessing narcotic drugs, and possessing drug paraphernalia.

In preparing for trial, the State sent the various drugs and drug-related items it had seized from the shed to an Arizona Department of Public Safety (DPS) crime lab for analysis. DPS analyst Elizabeth Rast determined and informed prosecutors of which items needed to be analyzed, performed the analysis, and recorded her findings in a set of typed notes and a signed report on DPS letterhead. Rast's two-page signed report conveyed her conclusions about the lab work and results contained in her typed notes. Rast's analysis centered on eight items, four of which she found "contained a usable quantity of methamphetamine," three "a usable quantity of marijuana," and one "a usable quantity of cannabis."[37]

Although the State had planned for Rast to testify about her findings at Smith's trial, it replaced Rast with Greggory Longoni, a different DPS analyst, three weeks before trial because "Rast had stopped working at the lab, for unexplained reasons."[38] "Longoni had no prior connection to the Smith case, and the State did not claim otherwise."[39] In his testimony, Longoni spoke about four of the items Rast analyzed, explaining the work Rast had done and her findings. He then offered an "independent opinion" about her findings where he relayed her ultimate conclusions that there were usable amounts of various drugs in each of the items he discussed.[40]

Smith was convicted and his conviction was upheld by the Arizona appellate courts. The Supreme Court unanimously reversed, but with many separate opinions. Justice Kagan wrote for the Court and said that the first step in analysis under the Confrontation Clause is whether Rast's statements were "introduced for their truth."[41]

The Court concluded that "Rast's statements . . . came in for their truth, and no less because they were admitted to show the basis of Longoni's expert opinions."[42] Justice Kagan observes that Longoni's testimony was only possible "because he accepted the truth of what Rast had reported about her work in the lab" and that "likewise, the jury could credit Longoni's opinions identifying the substances only because it too accepted the truth of what Rast reported about her lab work."[43] Rast's absence thus meant that Smith had no opportunity to question the veracity of the report upon which his entire conviction depended.

Justice Kagan explained that permitting the testimony would "allow for easy evasion of the Confrontation Clause."[44] Although expert witnesses like Longoni, who did not himself analyze anything, may answer hypothetical questions that speak to the ramifications that flow if assuming an out-of-court statement to be true, "the bulk of Longoni's testimony took no such permissible form"; he "effectively became Rast's mouthpiece" in relaying everything she reports having done.[45] Thus, "if the out-of-court statements were also testimonial, their admission violated the Confrontation Clause."[46] The Court said that the issue of whether the statements were testimonial was not before it and remanded the case.

Justice Thomas, in a concurring opinion, repeated his view from *Williams v. Illinois* that the Confrontation Clause "is implicated by extrajudicial statements only insofar as they are contained in formalized testimonial materials, such as affidavits, depositions, prior testimony, or confessions."[47] Justice Thomas said that on remand the court of appeals should focus on "whether the statements at issue have the requisite formality and solemnity to qualify as testimonial" and, if they do not, conclude there is no Confrontation Clause issue as to their admission.[48]

Justice Alito concurred in the judgment, joined by Chief Justice Roberts, but strongly disagreed with the majority. He said that "today, the Court inflicts a needless, unwarranted, and crippling wound on modern evidence law."[49] Justice Alito explained that no Confrontation Clause issue can be rightly raised if a jury is instructed that the evidence is not admitted for its truth. He argued that the Court is only able to address the Confrontation Clause issue by believing that juries are incapable of following instruction, "but that conclusion is inconsistent with commonplace trial practice" since juries routinely receive and follow a judge's instruction that evidence is admitted for limited purposes only.[50]

Smith curtails what expert witnesses can say without being subject to the Confrontation Clause. It resolves confusion created by *Williams v. Illinois* and takes a broad approach to defining when expert testimony is introduced for the "truth of the matter asserted."

Federal Criminal Laws

As always, there were many cases construing federal criminal statutes. Two seem particularly important: *Snyder v. United States*,[51] concerning the federal statute prohibiting bribery of state and local officials, and *Fischer v. United States*,[52] involving the federal law prohibiting interference with official proceedings.

Snyder v. United States. In a series of recent cases, the Supreme Court has narrowed the federal laws used in corruption and white collar criminal prosecutions.[53] For example, in *Skilling v. United States*, the Supreme Court narrowed the scope of the federal "honest services fraud" statute, narrowing it to include only bribes and kickbacks, but not fraud.[54] In *McDonnell v. United States*, the Court vacated the bribery convictions for the former governor of Virginia, narrowing the meaning of an "official act" under the bribery statute so that it did not include actions such as setting up a meeting, calling another public official, or hosting an event.[55]

Once more this term, in *Snyder v. United States*, the Court narrowly interpreted a federal criminal law meant to deal with corruption. The case involved a federal law—18 U.S.C. § 666(a)(1)(B)—that makes it a crime when an official "corruptly solicits or demands for the benefit of any person, or accepts or agrees to accept, anything of value from any person, intending to be influenced or rewarded in connection with any business, transaction, or series of transactions of such organization, government, or agency involving anything of value of $5,000 or more."

In 2013, Indiana's City of Portage awarded two contracts worth $1.1 million to Great Lakes Peterbilt, a local truck company, for the purchase of five trucks. The following year, Mayor James Snyder (who was also mayor when Portage awarded the contracts) received a $13,000 check from Peterbilt. Snyder claimed the $13,000 check was compensation for consulting services he had provided to Peterbilt, but "the FBI and federal prosecutors suspected that the payment was a gratuity for the City's trash truck contracts."[56] Snyder was charged and convicted of violating 18 U.S.C. § 666(a)(1)(B).

The Supreme Court, in a 6–3 decision split along ideological lines, reversed the conviction and held that there is fundamental distinction between illegal bribes and permissible gratuities and that the check paid to Snyder was a gratuity. Justice Brett Kavanaugh wrote for the conservative majority, while Justice Ketanji Brown Jackson wrote for the three liberal dissenters.

Justice Kavanaugh focused on the statutory language and concluded the federal law prohibited only bribes, meaning payments before an official act in order to influence the public official. He explained that the law did not criminalize gratuities, meaning payments after the official acts, so long as there is no quid pro quo. Put another way, the Court said that the statute does not make it a crime to give gratuities to state and local officials that are a "token of appreciation after the official act."[57]

Justice Jackson wrote a strong dissent and argued that § 666 was meant to prohibit gratuities as well as bribes. She, too, focused on the statutory language. She said that on its face, § 666's "use of the term 'influenced' captures *quid pro quo* bargains struck before an official act is taken—and therefore bribes," while "the term 'rewarded' easily covers the concept of gratuities paid to corrupt officials after the fact."[58]

Snyder is a blow to the government's ability to prosecute state and local officials for accepting gratuities under § 666, as it eliminates gratuities from the reach of the statute. This means that it falls on state and local governments to call their officials to task, if they have the legislation to do so. In *Snyder*'s case, Indiana did not have such a law. The case is also a message to state and local officials, and those who want to influence them: it is fine to give a gift after the government official's decision, even a large one, so long as there is not a quid pro quo. It also continues the Court's narrowing of federal laws that concern corruption and white collar crime.

Fischer v. United States. This was one of the more closely watched decisions of the term because it involved a federal statute that was used in the prosecution of those involved in the January 6 insurrection and is a basis for some of the counts of the indictment of Donald Trump in federal court in Washington, D.C.

Joseph Fischer took part in the events of January 6, 2021, at the U.S. Capitol. Fischer was among those who "'forced entry' into the building, 'breaking windows,' and 'assaulting members of the U.S. Capitol Police.'"[59] Fischer was indicted on seven counts by a grand jury, six of which alleged that he "forcibly assaulted a federal officer, entered and remained in a restricted building, and engaged in disorderly and disruptive conduct in the Capitol, among other crimes."[60]

The issue before the Court involved count three of the indictment, which charged Fischer with violating 18 U.S.C. § 1512(c)(2). This provision provides:

> (c) Whoever corruptly—
>
> > (1) alters, destroys, mutilates, or conceals a record, document, or other object, or attempts to do so, with the intent to impair the object's integrity or availability for use in an official proceeding; or
> >
> > (2) otherwise obstructs, influences, or impedes any official proceeding, or attempts to do so, shall be fined . . . or imprisoned not more than 20 years, or both.

The question before the Court was whether the second paragraph should be read to apply to any attempt to "obstruct, influence, or impede" an official proceeding or whether it should be construed narrowly to apply only when there is destruction of documents.

The Supreme Court, in a 6–3 decision, chose the latter and held that the meaning of § 1512(c)(2) is limited by the language of § 1512(c)(1) and thus only applies to actions relating to the integrity or availability of evidence at an official proceeding. There was an unusual split among justices. Chief Justice Roberts wrote the opinion for the Court, which was joined by Justices Thomas, Alito, Gorsuch, Kavanaugh, and

Jackson. Justice Barrett wrote the dissent, joined by Justices Sotomayor and Kagan.

Chief Justice Roberts stressed that subsection (c)(2) had to be interpreted in light of subsection (c)(1). He said that "[t]ethering (c)(2) to the context of (c)(1) recognizes the distinct purpose of each provision."[61] He explained that "subsection (c)(2) makes it a crime to impair the availability or integrity of records, documents, or objects used in an official proceeding in ways other than those specified in (c)(1)," such as by evidence falsification.[62] Further, subsection (c)(2) "ensures that liability is still imposed for impairing the availability or integrity of *other* things used in an official proceeding beyond" those enumerated in (c)(1).[63]

The Court further explained that because § 1512(c) was enacted specifically to address matters relating to evidence destruction, "it would be peculiar to conclude . . . Congress actually hid away in [§ 1512(c)(2)] a catchall provision that reaches far beyond the document shredding and similar scenarios that prompted the legislation in the first place."[64] The Court said that the "better conclusion is that subsection (c)(2) was designed by Congress to capture other forms of evidence and other means of impairing its integrity or availability beyond those Congress specified in (c)(1)."[65]

Justice Jackson wrote a concurring opinion stressing that this case was not about the immorality of the acts of those who took part in the events of January 6, 2021, but the "scope of the particular crime Congress has outlined in 18 U.S.C. §1512(c)(2)."[66]

Justice Barrett wrote a strong dissent. She said that § 1512(c)(2) is clear and that its language is not in any way limited to destruction of documents. She said that subsection (c)(2) "prohibits obstructing, influencing, or impeding an official proceeding by means *different* from those specified in (c)(1), thereby serving as a catchall."[67] Subsections (c)(1) and (c)(2) are similar in that "each crime represents one means through which to obstruct, influence, or impede an official proceeding."[68] Because Fischer's alleged participation in the January 6 riot "forced the delay of Congress's joint session," and "[b]locking an official proceeding from moving forward surely qualifies as obstructing or impeding the proceeding by means *other than* document destruction," "Fischer's alleged conduct thus falls within (c)(2)'s scope."[69]

The Court's decision significantly limits the scope of § 1512(c)(2). For Fischer, and others prosecuted for the events on January 6, it was just one of several laws used to indict and convict them. This decision overturns one of the convictions and may require resentencing, but all were convicted of other crimes as well. Likewise, for former President Trump it is only part of his indictment. And perhaps for both the January 6 defendants and for Trump there can be a showing that their actions obstructed access to documents. But the law is now clear that obstructing or impeding an official proceeding within the meaning of § 1512(c)(2) is limited to acts that obstruct, conceal, or destroy documents.

Sentencing

A number of federal statutes create mandatory minimum sentences. Drug possession is one type of crime where mandatory minimums apply. The exact minimum sentence imposed on a defendant convicted of drug possession depends "on the type and quantity of drug at issue, the harm resulting from the crime, and (relevant here) the defendant's criminal history."[70] Under 18 U.S.C. § 3553(f), certain defendants convicted of drug possession may be eligible for relief from mandatory minimum sentences. Eligibility for § 3553(f) relief is determined by looking at the characteristics of the offense, whether the defendant acted as a ringleader, and the defendant's relevant criminal history.

In 2020, Mark Pulsifer pled guilty to distributing at least 50 grams of methamphetamine, facing a mandatory minimum sentence of 15 years in prison unless eligible for safety-valve relief under § 3553(f). The portion of § 3553(f) in dispute is paragraph (f)(1), which pertains to the criminal history of the defendant seeking relief. It establishes that judges may exercise discretion without regard to mandatory minimums when

> (1) the defendant does not have—
>
> > (A) more than 4 criminal history points, excluding any criminal history points resulting from a 1-point offense, as determined under the sentencing guidelines;

> (B) a prior 3-point offense, as determined under the sentencing guidelines; and
>
> (C) a prior 2-point violent offense, as determined under the sentencing guidelines.

The question before the Court was whether *all* of these requirements had to be met for the safety-valve relief provision to apply. The Court said yes, in an opinion by Justice Elena Kagan. She wrote: "A defendant is eligible for safety-valve relief under paragraph (f)(1) only if he 'does not have' all three of the items listed—or said more specifically, does not have four criminal-history points, does not have a prior three-point offense, and does not have a prior two-point violent offense. The paragraph thus creates an eligibility checklist, and demands that a defendant satisfy every one of its conditions."[71]

Justice Gorsuch dissented, joined by Justices Sotomayor and Jackson. He noted that Congress sought to reduce incarceration and lessen the harshness of mandatory minimum sentence laws. He said that paragraph (f)(1) should be interpreted as meaning that defendants are eligible for safety-valve release so long as they do not have the entire combination of subparagraph A, B, *and* C. Unlike the majority, which argues that "and" should be read as meaning "or," Justice Gorsuch invokes the "meaningful-variation canon," which understands that "when Congress uses different terms in a statute, we normally presume it does so to convey different meanings."[72]

Pulsifer makes safety-valve eligibility much harder to obtain for defendants with prior criminal history, since should their criminal history contain any of the features of subparagraphs A, B, or C, they are now ineligible for relief and are subject to mandatory minimums. Drawing on the statistics cited by Justice Gorsuch, the real-world effect of *Pulsifer* is that the revised version of § 3553(f), which was meant to increase access to safety-valve relief, only increases relief from 33 percent to 44 percent of inmates, rather than to 66 percent, as would have been had under Pulsifer's reading of the statute.[73]

Endnotes

1. Erlinger v. United States, 144 S. Ct. 1840 (2024).
2. Apprendi v. New Jersey, 530 U.S. 466 (2000).
3. Almendarez-Torres v. United States, 523 U.S. 224 (1998).
4. *Erlinger*, 144 S. Ct. at 1846.
5. *Id.*
6. *Id.*
7. *Id.* at 1847.
8. *Id.*
9. *Id.*
10. *Id.*
11. Erlinger v. United States, No. 2:19-cv-00518-JMS-MJD, 2021 U.S. Dist. LEXIS 129075 (S.D. Ind. July 12, 2021).
12. *Erlinger*, 144 S. Ct. at 1847.
13. United States v. Erlinger, 77 F.4th 617 (7th Cir. 2023).
14. *Erlinger*, 144 S. Ct. at 1850.
15. *Id.* at 1853.
16. *Id.* at 1853-54.
17. *Id.* at 1854.
18. *Id.* at 1855.
19. *Id.* at 1856.
20. *Id.* at 1859.
21. *Id.*
22. *Id.*
23. *Id.* at 1861 (Thomas, J., concurring).
24. *Id.*
25. *Id.* at 1862 (Kavanaugh, J., dissenting).
26. *Id.*
27. *Id.* at 1867.
28. *Id.* at 1873.
29. *Id.* at 1878 (Jackson, J., dissenting).
30. *Id.* at 1880.
31. *Id.* at 1880-81.
32. Crawford v. Washington, 541 U.S. 36 (2004).
33. Melendez-Diaz v. Massachusetts, 557 U.S. 305 (2009).
34. Bullcoming v. New Mexico, 546 U.S. 647 (2011).
35. Williams v. Illinois, 567 U.S. 50 (2012).

36. Smith v. Arizona, 144 S. Ct. 1785 (2024).
37. *Id.* at 1795.
38. *Id.*
39. *Id.*
40. *Id.* at 1796.
41. *Id.* at 1797.
42. *Id.* at 1799.
43. *Id.* at 1799-1800.
44. *Id.* at 1800.
45. *Id.* at 1800-01.
46. *Id.* at 1801.
47. *Id.* at 1803 (Thomas, J., concurring in the judgment).
48. *Id.* at 1803-04.
49. *Id.* at 1805 (Alito, J., concurring in the judgment).
50. *Id.* at 1809.
51. Snyder v. United States, 144 S. Ct. 1947 (2024).
52. Fischer v. United States, 144 S. Ct. 2176 (2024).
53. *See* Jeff Chemerinsky, *Supreme Court Decision Weakens Federal Corruption on Local Officials*, Daily J., July 12, 2024.
54. Skilling v. United States, 561 U.S. 358 (2010).
55. McDonnell v. United States, 579 U.S. 550 (2016).
56. *Snyder*, 144 S. Ct. at 1954.
57. *Id.* at 1951.
58. *Id.* at 1962 (Jackson, J., dissenting).
59. Fischer v. United States, 144 S. Ct. 2176, 2182 (2024).
60. *Id.*
61. *Id.* at 2185.
62. *Id.* at 2186.
63. *Id.*
64. *Id.*
65. *Id.*
66. *Id.* at 2190 (Jackson, J., concurring).
67. *Id.* at 2195 (Barrett, J., dissenting).
68. *Id.*
69. *Id.*
70. Pulsifer v. United States, 144 S. Ct. 718, 723 (2024).
71. *Id.* at 725.
72. *Id.* at 742 (Gorsuch, J., dissenting).
73. *Id.* at 741–42.

7

Eighth Amendment

Can a city make it a crime for unhoused individuals to sleep in public if there are not other places for them to go? In *City of Grants Pass v. Johnson*, the Supreme Court, in a 6–3 decision, held that it does not violate the Eighth Amendment for a city to enforce an anticamping ordinance that makes it a crime to sleep in public even if there are not adequate shelter beds for the homeless.[1]

Martin v. City of Boise

The Ninth Circuit's decision in *Johnson v. City of Grants Pass* was based on its earlier ruling in *Martin v. City of Boise*, in 2018.[2] Boise, Idaho enacted an ordinance that made it a misdemeanor to use "any of the streets, sidewalks, parks, or public places as a camping place at any time." The camping ordinance defined "camping" as "the use of public property as a temporary or permanent place of dwelling, lodging, or residence."[3]

The Ninth Circuit, in an opinion by Judge Marsha Berzon, found that it was cruel and unusual punishment to impose criminal penalties on homeless individuals for sleeping in public if there were not adequate shelter beds. The court relied on *Robinson v. California*, a 1962 Supreme

Court decision, which declared unconstitutional a California statute that "ma[de] the 'status' of narcotic addiction a criminal offense."[4] The Supreme Court explained that the California law was "not one which punishe[d] a person for the use of narcotics, for their purchase, sale or possession, or for antisocial or disorderly behavior resulting from their administration"; it punished addiction itself.[5] The Court explained that the Eighth Amendment limits the conduct that the government may punish: "Even one day in prison would be a cruel and unusual punishment for the 'crime' of having a common cold."[6]

The Ninth Circuit explained that everyone must sleep and concluded that it violates the Eighth Amendment to punish sleeping in public when a person has no place else to sleep. The court explained: "We hold only that 'so long as there is a greater number of homeless individuals in [a jurisdiction] than the number of available beds [in shelters],' the jurisdiction cannot prosecute homeless individuals for involuntarily sitting, lying, and sleeping in public. That is, as long as there is no option of sleeping indoors, the government cannot criminalize indigent, homeless people for sleeping outdoors, on public property, on the false premise they had a choice in the matter."[7]

Johnson v. City of Grants Pass in the Ninth Circuit

Grants Pass is a city in Oregon with a population of about 39,000 and a homeless population that may be as many as 600. As the Ninth Circuit explained, "[T]he number of homeless persons outnumber [*sic*] the available shelter beds. In other words, homeless persons have nowhere to shelter and sleep in the City other than on the streets or in parks."[8]

Grants Pass adopted a series of ordinances meant to keep unhoused individuals from sleeping on public property. One ordinance provides, "No person may sleep on public sidewalks, streets, or alleyways at any time as a matter of individual and public safety. No person may sleep in any pedestrian or vehicular entrance to public or private property abutting a public sidewalk." Another ordinance prohibited persons from occupying a "campsite" on all public property, such as parks, benches, or rights of way. The term "campsite" was defined as any place "where bedding, sleeping bag, or other material [is] used for bedding purposes." As the Ninth Circuit observed, "City ordinances preclude homeless persons from using a blanket, a pillow, or a cardboard box for protection from the elements while sleeping within the City's limits."[9] The ordinances provide for civil fines, exclusion orders from city property for repeat violations, and criminal penalties for violating exclusion orders.

The Ninth Circuit, in an opinion by Judge Roslyn Silver, concluded: "[T]he City of Grants Pass cannot, consistent with the Eighth Amendment, enforce its anti-camping ordinances against homeless persons for the mere act of sleeping outside with rudimentary protection from the elements or for sleeping in their car at night, when there is no other place in the City for them to go."[10]

The Ninth Circuit, by a vote of 14–13, denied en banc review. Every court of appeals judge appointed by a Democratic president voted against en banc review, while every judge appointed by a Republican president voted in favor of en banc review.

Supreme Court's Decision

In a deeply divided 6–3 decision, the Supreme Court reversed the Ninth Circuit. Justice Neil Gorsuch wrote for the six conservative justices and Justice Sonia Sotomayor wrote for the three liberal dissenters. Quite significantly, the Court gave a narrow reading to the scope of the Eighth Amendment, saying: "The Cruel and Unusual Punishments Clause focuses on the question what 'method or kind of punishment' a government may impose after a criminal conviction, not on the question whether a government may criminalize particular behavior in the first place or how it may go about securing a conviction for that offense."[11] That seems in clear tension with *Robinson v. California*, which said that the Eighth Amendment also limits what conduct can constitutionally be punished. But the Court did not overrule *Robinson v. California* and said, "[N]o one has asked us to reconsider *Robinson*. Nor do we see any need to do so today."[12]

The Court invoked *Powell v. Texas*, a 1968 case that upheld punishing public drunkenness, and said that it supports the ability of the government to punish conduct as opposed to a status.[13] The Court said that Grants Pass was punishing the conduct of camping in public, not the status of a person being homeless. The Court explained that nothing prevents the government from punishing involuntary acts and besides, "how are city officials and law enforcement officers to know what it means to be 'involuntarily' homeless, or whether any particular person meets that standard?"[14]

Justice Gorsuch concluded his majority opinion by describing the limited role of the federal courts in this area: "Homelessness is complex. Its causes are many. So may be the public policy responses required to address it. At bottom, the question this case presents is whether the Eighth Amendment grants federal judges primary responsibility for assessing those causes and devising those responses. It does not."[15]

Justice Thomas wrote a concurring opinion saying that *Robinson v. California* was incorrectly decided and should be overruled.[16] He also said that the primary focus of the Grants Pass ordinances was to create civil liability, something not covered by the Eighth Amendment's cruel and unusual punishment clause.

Justice Sotomayor wrote a blistering dissenting opinion, joined by Justices Kagan and Jackson. In her first paragraph she expressed her strong disagreement with the Court's majority: "Sleep is a biological necessity, not a crime. For some people, sleeping outside is their only option. The City of Grants Pass jails and fines those people for sleeping anywhere in public at any time, including in their cars, if they use as little as a blanket to keep warm or a rolled-up shirt as a pillow. For people with no access to shelter, that punishes them for being homeless. That is unconscionable and unconstitutional. Punishing people for their status is 'cruel and unusual' under the Eighth Amendment."[17]

Justice Sotomayor noted that 600,000 people are homeless in the United States on any given night and that they are unhoused for many different reasons.[18] She said that the Grants Pass ordinances punish the status of being homeless because absent adequate shelter beds, unhoused individuals have nowhere else to sleep. She powerfully declared: "It is possible to acknowledge and balance the issues facing local governments, the humanity and dignity of homeless people, and our constitutional principles. Instead, the majority focuses almost exclusively on the needs of local governments and leaves the most vulnerable in our society with an impossible choice: Either stay awake or be arrested."[19]

Implications

The Court's decision is important in determining both the meaning of the Eighth Amendment and what cities can do as to homelessness and for the lives of those who are unhoused. As for the Eighth Amendment, the Court says it is not a limit on the conduct that can be punished. If the Court follows this, it would be a significant change in the law, as the Court said in *Ingraham v. Wright* that the Eighth Amendment "imposes substantive limits on what can be made criminal and punished as such."[20]

As for the unhoused, the Court makes clear that cities can choose to use their criminal laws. But nothing in the opinion requires that cities do so. No city is going to solve homelessness by criminally prosecuting the unhoused. Imposing fines that they cannot pay or putting them in jail for brief times is not going to take them off the street. Using criminal law to force the unhoused out of some cities will just move them elsewhere.

It is impossible to contemplate this case without thinking of the words of Anatole France: "The law, in its majestic equality, forbids rich and poor alike to sleep under bridges, to beg in the streets, and to steal their bread."[21]

Endnotes

1. City of Grants Pass v. Johnson, 144 S. Ct. 2202 (2024).
2. Martin v. City of Boise, 902 F.3d 1031 (9th Cir. 2018).
3. Boise City Code § 9-10-02.
4. Robinson v. California, 370 U.S. 666 (1962).
5. *Id.*
6. *Id.* at 667.
7. *Martin*, 902 F.3d at 1048.

8. Johnson v. City of Grants Pass, 72 F.4th 868, 874 (9th Cir. 2023).
9. *Id.* at 874–875.
10. *Id.* at 896.
11. City of Grants Pass v. Johnson, 144 S. Ct. 2202, 2216 (2024).
12. *Id.* at 2218.
13. *Id.* at 2219 (citing Powell v. Texas, 382 U.S. 514 (1968)).
14. *Id.* at 2221.
15. *Id.* at 2226.
16. *Id.* at 2226 (Thomas, J., concurring).
17. *Id.* at 2228 (Sotomayor, J., dissenting).
18. *Id.* at 2229.
19. *Id.* at 2228.
20. Ingraham v. Wright, 430 U.S. 651 (1977).
21. Anatole France, The Red Lily (1894).

8

Employment and Labor Law

Employment Discrimination

The Court decided one important case concerning the scope of the federal law prohibiting discrimination in employment: *Muldrow v. City of St. Louis*.[1] The issue is what injury is required in order for a plaintiff to bring a claim for employment discrimination under Title VII of the 1964 Civil Rights Act. The Court held that an employee challenging a job transfer under Title VII must show that the transfer brought about some harm with respect to an identifiable term or condition of employment, but that harm need not be significant.

Jatonya Muldrow was a sergeant in the St. Louis, Missouri Police Department. From 2008 to 2017, she was assigned to the Intelligence Division. During this time, she investigated public corruption and human trafficking cases, oversaw the Gang Unit, and served as head of the Gun Crimes Unit. In this capacity, she worked closely with the Federal Bureau of Investigation—"a status granting her, among other things, FBI credentials, an unmarked take-home vehicle, and the authority to pursue investigations outside St. Louis."[2] She was praised for her service.

In 2017, a new commander of the Intelligence Division asked that Muldrow be transferred in order to replace her with a male police officer. He later testified that he felt that a man "seemed a better fit for the Division's 'very dangerous' work."[3] The transfer occurred over Muldrow's objections.

Muldrow suffered no loss of pay or rank. But there was a significant change in her responsibilities, perks, and schedule. She was supervising patrol officers and sometimes on patrol herself. She lost her FBI credentials and the car that came with them. Also, she often had to work weekends in the new position, whereas the prior job was primarily Mondays through Fridays.

Muldrow sued under Title VII of the 1964 Civil Rights Act claiming sex discrimination. She said that the department had "discriminate[d] against" her based on sex "with respect to" the "terms [or] conditions" of her employment.

The federal district court ruled against her and the U.S. Court of Appeals affirmed. Both said that Muldrow had to—but could not—show that the transfer caused a "materially significant disadvantage."[4] Both stressed that she had not suffered any loss of salary or rank and thus did not have a sufficient harm for a claim under Title VII.

The Supreme Court, in an opinion by Justice Elena Kagan, unanimously reversed. The Court reaffirmed that there must be a harm to the plaintiff in order to bring a Title VII claim, but it need not be "economic or tangible."[5] Justice Kagan said: "To make out a Title VII discrimination claim, a transferee must show some harm respecting an identifiable term or condition of employment."[6]

But the Court rejected the lower courts' view that the harm had to be significant in order for there to be a claim under Title VII. The Court declared: "What the transferee does not have to show, according to the relevant text, is that the harm incurred was 'significant.' Or serious, or substantial, or any similar adjective suggesting that the disadvantage to the employee must exceed a heightened bar. 'Discriminate against' means treat worse, here based on sex. But neither that phrase nor any other says anything about how much worse."[7] The Court stressed that to add "significant" is to create a requirement not found in the statutory language of Title VII.

The Court was explicit that the lower courts in this case had used the wrong legal standard. It stated: "Muldrow need show only some injury respecting her employment terms or conditions. The transfer must have left her worse off, but need not have left her significantly so. And Muldrow's allegations, if properly preserved and supported, meet that test with room to spare. . . . Title VII prohibits making a transfer, based on sex, with the consequences Muldrow described."[8]

Justices Thomas, Alito, and Kavanaugh each wrote separate opinions. Justice Thomas concurred and said that he thought that the Court's opinion mischaracterized the Eighth Circuit's approach to Title VII.[9]

Justice Alito concurred in the judgment, but in language that sounded more like a dissent. He said: "I do not join the Court's unhelpful opinion. . . . I see little if any substantive difference between the terminology the Court approves and the terminology it doesn't like. The predictable result of today's decision is that careful lower court judges will mind the words they use but will continue to do pretty much just what they have done for years."[10]

Justice Kavanaugh also concurred in the judgment and would have adopted a simpler approach than the majority. He said that a "transfer made on the basis of the employee's race, color, religion, sex, or national origin violates Title VII."[11] He said that he "disagree[d] with the Court's new some-harm requirement."[12] He said that no court had adopted such an approach and that it was unclear what it would mean in practice. He concluded, though, that in practice there was little difference between his approach and that of the majority: "Therefore, anyone who has been transferred because of race, color, religion, sex, or national origin should easily be able to show some additional harm—whether in money, time, satisfaction, schedule, convenience, commuting costs or time, prestige, status, career prospects, interest level, perks, professional relationships, networking opportunities, effects on family obligations, or the like. So even though I respectfully disagree with the Court's new some-harm requirement, I expect that the Court's approach and my preferred approach will land in the same place and lead to the same result in 99 out of 100 discriminatory-transfer cases, if not in all 100."[13]

The case is important in clarifying what an employment discrimination plaintiff must allege and prove, and also what a court must find for a Title VII claim. There must be an allegation of some harm, but it need not be monetary or tangible or significant. As Justice Kavanaugh said, this should be an easy standard for most plaintiffs to meet.

Labor Law

In *Starbucks Corp. v. McKinney*, the Court considered the standard courts should use in deciding whether to grant a preliminary injunction to the National Labor Relations Board under the National Labor Relations Act.[14] In 2022, six employees at a Memphis, Tennessee Starbucks store announced plans to unionize the store and formed an organizing committee. Some employees invited a local television station to visit the store after hours and gave interviews about their plans to unionize.

Starbucks, after learning of this, fired the employees involved with the media event for violating company policy. These included the members of the union organizing committee who were in attendance. The union coordinating with the employees filed charges with the board.

The union filed a grievance with the National Labor Relations Board. After investigating the allegations, the board issued a complaint against Starbucks. The regional director then sought a preliminary injunction—known as a § 10(j) petition—in the U.S. District Court for the Western District of Tennessee. The requested preliminary injunction would, among other things, require Starbucks to reinstate the fired employees. Section 10(j) of the National Labor Relations Act provides that, "upon issuance of a complaint," the board may "petition any United States district court . . . for appropriate temporary relief." A district court considering a § 10(j) petition may "grant to the Board such temporary relief . . . as it deems just and proper."

The district court issued a preliminary injunction and the U.S. Court of Appeals for the Sixth Circuit affirmed. Both applied a two-part test that focused on whether "there is reasonable cause to believe that unfair labor practices have occurred" and whether injunctive relief is "just and proper."[15]

The Supreme Court reversed in an opinion by Justice Clarence Thomas. The Court said that it had prescribed a four-part test for courts to use in evaluating whether to grant a preliminary injunction. The Court explained that there was no reason to depart from this usual approach for § 10(j) petitions. Under the four-part test, a party "seeking a preliminary injunction must make a clear showing that 'he is likely to succeed on the merits, that he is likely to suffer irreparable harm in the absence of preliminary relief, that the balance of equities tips in his favor, and that an injunction is in the public interest.'"[16] The Court declared: "Nothing in § 10(j)'s text overcomes the presumption that the four traditional criteria govern a preliminary-injunction request by the Board."[17]

Justice Jackson wrote an opinion concurring in part, concurring in the judgment, and dissenting in part. She said that § 10(j) was meant to constrain the courts given "an ignominious history of abuse" of injunctions against union activity by federal courts.[18]

She said that the majority failed to recognize that injunctions under § 10(j) are different given Congress's purpose in the National Labor Relations Act. She wrote: "A petition for § 10(j) relief serves a straightforward, but significant purpose: 'to preserve the NLRB's remedial power while the Board resolves an unfair labor practice charge.' . . . In doing so, 'the Court unnecessarily and casually substitutes the chancellor's clumsy foot for the rule of law.' I am loath to bless this aggrandizement of judicial power where Congress has so plainly limited the discretion of the courts, and where it so clearly intends for the expert agency it has created to make the primary determinations about both merits and process."[19]

Interestingly, a year ago, in *Glacier Northwest, Inc. v. International Brotherhood of Teamsters Local No. 174*, the Court also ruled against a union in an 8–1 decision with Justice Jackson as the sole dissent.[20] In her short time on the Court, she has emerged as a powerful voice for labor.

Endnotes

1. Muldrow v. City of St. Louis, 144 S. Ct. 967 (2024).
2. *Id.* at 972.
3. *Id.*
4. Muldrow v. City of St. Louis, 30 F.4th 680, 688 (2022).
5. *Muldrow*, 144 S. Ct. at 974 (citing Oncale v. Sundowner Offshore Servs., Inc., 523 U.S. 75, 78 (1998)).
6. *Id.* at 974.
7. *Id.*
8. *Id.* at 977.
9. *Id.* (Thomas, J., concurring).
10. *Id.* at 978–79 (Alito, J., concurring in the judgment).
11. *Id.* at 979 (Kavanaugh, J., concurring in the judgment).
12. *Id.* at 980.
13. *Id.*
14. Starbucks Corp. v. McKinney, 144 S. Ct. 1570 (2024).
15. McKinney v. Starbucks Corp., 77 F.4th 391 (6th Cir. 2023); McKinney v. Starbucks Corp., No. 2:22-cv-2292-SHL-CGC, 2022 WL 5434206 (W.D. Tenn. Aug. 18, 2022).
16. *Starbucks Corp.*, 144 S. Ct. at 1576 (citations omitted).
17. *Id.*
18. *Id.* at 1581.
19. *Id.* at 1587–88.
20. Glacier Nw., Inc. v. Int'l Bhd. of Teamsters Local No. 174, 143 S. Ct. 1404 (2023).

9

The First Amendment: Freedom of Speech and Freedom of the Press

The Court had a number of cases posing important issues about the First Amendment's protection of freedom of speech and the press. Several involved issues concerning social media and the internet. But the Court did not reach many of these questions, sometimes dismissing cases and sometimes ruling narrowly. Even when the Court decided, their rulings seemed to leave as many questions as they provided answers.

Government Officials' Social Media Accounts

If a government official has a social media account and discusses government business on it, is the First Amendment violated if the official removes critical comments or blocks critics from having continued access? This arose when Donald Trump was president and blocked some of his critics from having access to his Twitter account. Both the federal district court and the U.S. Court of Appeals for the Second Circuit ruled against Trump, but the Supreme Court dismissed the case as moot because when the case reached them, Trump was no longer president.[1]

The issue arises, though, at all levels of government and ultimately is one of state action: does the First Amendment apply to social media accounts of government officials where government business is discussed? That was the question in *Lindke v. Freed*.[2] James Freed is the city manager of Port Huron, Michigan. He has a Facebook page where he posts family pictures and news. He also regularly posted information regarding his job and matters concerning city government.

Kevin Lindke is a resident of Port Huron and a constituent. Lindke posted negative comments about Freed on Freed's Facebook page. Freed deleted Lindke's critical comments and then blocked Lindke's ability to post in the future. Lindke sued Freed for violating the First Amendment. The U.S. Court of Appeals for the Sixth Circuit concluded that there was not state action and therefore the First Amendment did not apply.[3]

The U.S. Supreme Court reversed and remanded the case for further consideration. Justice Amy Coney Barrett wrote the opinion for a unanimous Court. She said that the fact that Freed is a government official alone is not sufficient for the First Amendment to apply. Determining whether or not the First Amendment applies requires further analysis. She explained: "Private parties can act with the authority of the State, and state officials have private lives and their own constitutional rights."[4]

The Court adopted a two-part test for determining if there is state action and thus if the First Amendment applies to government officials' social media accounts. Justice Barrett wrote: "[A] public official's social-media activity constitutes state action under § 1983 only if the official (1) possessed actual authority to speak on the State's behalf, and (2) purported to exercise that authority when he spoke on social media. The appearance and function of the social-media activity are relevant at the second step, but they cannot make up for a lack of state authority at the first."[5]

The Supreme Court has thus provided lower courts and litigants a test that they can apply. But this two-part test provides much less guidance than it may seem. As for the first prong, how is it to be decided whether a government official has the authority to speak for the government? Justice Barrett said that "[d]etermining the scope of an official's power requires careful attention to the relevant statute, ordinance, regulation, custom, or usage. In some cases, a grant of authority over particular subject matter may reasonably encompass authority to speak about it officially."[6]

But this still leaves great ambiguity. I am dean of the University of California, Berkeley School of Law. It is unclear as to when, if at all, I can speak for the law school. Arguably, only the regents of the University of California can speak for the university or any of its units. Or it can be argued that only the chancellor can speak for the Berkeley campus.

As for the second requirement, how is it to be decided when someone is speaking for the government? When I write an op-ed, or for that matter this book, it identifies me by title. Is that enough for me to be speaking for the government?

It is worth noting that at the end of the opinion, Justice Barrett said that there might be a significant difference between a public official removing critical comments and a public official blocking someone's access to a social media account. Justice Barrett wrote: "The nature of the technology matters to the state-action analysis. Freed performed two actions to which Lindke objected: He deleted Lindke's comments and blocked him from commenting again. So far as deletion goes, the only relevant posts are those from which Lindke's comments were removed. Blocking, however, is a different story. Because blocking operated on a page-wide basis, a court would have to consider whether Freed had engaged in state action with respect to any post on which Lindke wished to comment."[7]

Justice Barrett concluded by giving advice to public officials: they can avoid First Amendment obstacles by not discussing government business on their private social media accounts. She said: "A public official who fails to keep personal posts in a clearly designated personal account therefore exposes himself to greater potential liability."[8]

Speech by Government Officials as an Infringement of the Speech of Others

As a dean of a public university law school, do I violate my students' free speech rights when I encourage them to speak respectfully to one another, to demonstrate civility, and to refrain from hateful expression? I have had students object that my saying that chills their speech. If I condemn expression as racist or anti-Semitic or Islamophobic—even if no sanctions are imposed—am I impermissibly chilling speech?

There are countless instances in which government officials speak out, but those who disagree claim that it is chilling their freedom of expression and claim a First Amendment violation. In two cases this term the Supreme Court has reaffirmed that such speech by government officials violates the First Amendment only if there is an explicit threat of sanctions being imposed.

The Supreme Court has rarely dealt with this issue. In *Bantam Books, Inc. v. Sullivan*, in 1963, the Court held that it was unconstitutional for the Rhode Island Commission to Encourage Morality in Youth to identify "objectionable" books they claimed were unsuitable for children and to write to sellers urging them to stop selling those books.[9] The letter also informed the recipient that the commission recommended obscenity prosecutions to prosecutors and turned over its list of distributors of objectionable books to local police. Additionally, a police officer often followed up and visited the recipient of a letter to see what actions had been taken in response to the letter. The Supreme Court found such pressure to be an unconstitutional prior restraint of speech, even though no books were actually banned and no prosecutions were undertaken.

This term, in *National Rifle Association of America v. Vullo*, the Court applied *Bantam Books v. Sullivan* to allow a suit by the NRA against Maria Vullo, who had been the superintendent of the New York Department of Financial Services (DFS).[10] After the Parkland, Florida school shooting, which killed 17 students and staff members, Vullo allegedly encouraged insurance companies and bank officials, whom she regulated, to no longer do business with the NRA. The complaint alleges Vullo agreed not to prosecute the companies for their violations of the law if they ended their financial relationships with the NRA.

The Supreme Court in a unanimous decision found that the NRA presented a claim under the First Amendment. It is crucial to note that the case was at the motion-to-dismiss stage where the Court had to accept the allegations of the complaint as true. Justice Sonia Sotomayor wrote for a unanimous Court and said that it was reaffirming *Bantam Books v. Sullivan*: "Government officials cannot attempt to coerce private parties in order to punish or suppress views that the government disfavors."[11] Justice Sotomayor explained: "To state a claim that the government violated the First Amendment through coercion of a third party, a plaintiff must plausibly allege conduct that, viewed in context, could be reasonably understood to convey a threat of adverse government action in order to punish or suppress the plaintiff's speech. Accepting the well-pleaded factual allegations in the complaint as true, the NRA plausibly alleged that Vullo violated the First Amendment by coercing DFS-regulated entities into disassociating with the NRA in order to punish or suppress the NRA's gun-promotion advocacy."[12]

In other words, it is a threat of legal sanctions, or the promise of withholding sanctions, that makes speech by government officials a violation of the First Amendment. In this way, *National Rifle Association v. Vullo* is explicit that it is applying *Bantam Books v. Sullivan*.

Murthy v. Missouri also involved the question of when speech by government officials infringes the First Amendment, but this case was dismissed on standing grounds.[13] *Murthy v. Missouri* was a suit brought by two state governments and five social media users against the Biden administration and many federal agencies claiming that the government violated the First Amendment when it encouraged social media platforms to take down false speech. Unlike in *Bantam Books* and *NRA v. Vullo*, the government did not threaten social media platforms with prosecution. Rather, it told them that if they did not take down false speech—especially about the effects of the COVID-19 vaccines and the 2020 presidential election—they would face more regulation in the future.

A conservative federal district court judge in Louisiana ruled in favor of the plaintiffs and issued an injunction against the White House and many federal agencies. The Fifth Circuit reversed the injunction against the National Institute of Allergy and Infectious Diseases, the Cybersecurity and Infrastructure Agency, and the State Department. But the court of appeals left much of the injunction in place and said that the federal government coerced and encouraged platforms to remove false speech.

In a 6–3 decision, with the majority opinion written by Justice Amy Coney Barrett, the Court reversed the Fifth Circuit and ordered the case dismissed for lack of standing. In order for a plaintiff to have standing to sue in federal court, the plaintiff must show that he or she has been injured, that the injury was caused by the defendant, and that a favorable court decision is likely to remedy the harm.

The Court said that none of the plaintiffs could show that social media companies took down false speech because of coercion from the government. The Court stressed that "platforms had independent incentives to moderate content and often exercised their own judgment."[14] Justice Barrett wrote: "To be sure, the record reflects that the Government defendants played a role in at least some of the platforms' moderation choices. But the Fifth Circuit, by attributing *every* platform decision at least in part to the defendants, glossed over complexities in the evidence."[15]

Although the decision is based on standing, it has crucial implications for the First Amendment. Indeed, Justice Samuel Alito, in his dissent, described this as "one of the most important free speech cases to reach this Court in years."[16] Justice Alito, joined by Justices Thomas and Gorsuch, concluded that the pressure from government officials clearly violated the First Amendment. He said that dismissing the case on standing grounds was "regrettable."[17] He wrote: "What the officials did in this case was more subtle than the ham-handed censorship found to be unconstitutional in *Vullo*, but it was no less coercive. And because of the perpetrators' high positions, it was even more dangerous. It was blatantly unconstitutional, and the country may come to regret the Court's failure to say so. Officials who read today's decision together with *Vullo* will get the message. If a coercive campaign is carried out with enough sophistication, it may get by. That is not a message this Court should send."[18]

The premise of the Court's decision is that social media companies are private entities and can decide for themselves what speech to carry and what to remove. Government speech encouraging that they remove false speech only violates the First Amendment if it can be proven that the government caused, and will cause in the future, the blocking of speech.

The two recent decisions—*NRA v. Vullo* and *Murthy v. Missouri*—are important because they establish that the speech of government officials violates the First Amendment only if it is coercive and only if it can be proven to cause harm. It means that I, as a dean, need not fear a First Amendment claim for encouraging responsible speech by my students.

State Laws Prohibiting Content Moderation by Social Media Platforms

The two cases that had the possibility of being the most important with regard to the First Amendment—and perhaps the most significant ever with regard to social media—were *Moody v. NetChoice* and *NetChoice v. Paxton*. These cases were briefed and argued separately, though there was one opinion from the Court about both. Although the Court said that it was not deciding them, it gave some clear guidance to the lower courts and an indication of what it is likely to do when the issue returns to the Court (as it surely will).

Florida and Texas adopted laws prohibiting social media platforms from engaging in content moderation.[19] Each state did so on the ground that it believed that social media platforms disproportionately removed or blocked conservative viewpoints more than liberal ones. The laws were different in their scope and application, though motivated by the same concern. The Florida statute, S.B. 7072, applies to platforms with annual gross revenues of greater than $100 million and more than 100 million global monthly users.[20] This is clearly directed at the major social media platforms, like Facebook, TikTok, and Instagram. It contains five anti-censorship provisions, all of which have been preliminarily enjoined.[21] The Florida law prohibits "willfully deplatform[ing] a candidate for office."[22] It also prohibits a platform from "censor[ing], deplatform[ing], or shadow ban[ning] a journalistic enterprise based on the content of its publication or broadcast," unless that content is obscene.[23] It also requires that those whose posts have been removed be given notice.

Texas's anticensorship law, H.B. 20, is similar. The Texas law regulates any social media platform having over 50 million monthly active users that allows its users "to communicate with other users for the primary purpose of posting information, comments, messages, or images." It flatly prohibits "social media platforms"[24] from "censor[ing]" a "user's expression, or a user's ability to receive the expression of another person" on the basis of viewpoint or geographical location.[25] This is true even if the viewpoint is not expressed on the social media platform—that is, platforms cannot remove users or their posts on the basis of things said elsewhere.[26] The Texas law also requires that "concurrently with the removal" of user content, the platform shall "notify the user" and "explain the reason the content was removed." The user gets a right of appeal, and the platform must address an appeal within 14 days.

The U.S. Court of Appeals for the Eleventh Circuit declared the Florida law unconstitutional,[27] while the U.S. Court of Appeals for the Fifth Circuit upheld the Texas law.[28] The Supreme Court granted certiorari to resolve the conflict between the circuits.

The Court, though, did not decide the constitutionality of these laws, but instead remanded the cases. Although the Court was unanimous in its result in *Moody v. NetChoice*, there were five different opinions. Justice Kagan wrote for the majority. She said that NetChoice had brought facial challenges to the Florida and Texas laws. Justice Kagan explained the test for a facial challenge under the First Amendment: the question is whether "a substantial number of [the law's] applications are unconstitutional, judged in relation to the statute's plainly legitimate sweep. So in this singular context, even a law with 'a plainly legitimate sweep' may be struck down in its entirety. But that is so only if the law's unconstitutional applications substantially outweigh its constitutional ones."[29]

Justice Kagan said that the lower courts focused on some prominent applications, such as Facebook's News Feed and YouTube's homepage. But this is not sufficient for a facial analysis. She explained that the lower courts "did not address the full range of activities the laws cover, and measure the constitutional against the unconstitutional applications. In short, they treated these cases more like as-applied claims than like facial ones."[30] On remand, the lower courts need to consider the full sweep of these laws in determining whether their unconstitutional applications substantially outweigh the constitutional ones.

Interestingly, Justice Kagan did not stop there. She went on and made clear that the Fifth Circuit had erred in its analysis. The Fifth Circuit had treated social media platforms as common carriers and stressed the importance of regulation to ensure a diversity of views. Justice Kagan said that this rested "on a serious misunderstanding of First Amendment precedent and principle. The Fifth Circuit was wrong in concluding that Texas's restrictions on the platforms' selection, ordering, and labeling of third-party posts do not interfere with expression."[31]

Justice Kagan stressed that even though these are relatively new media, basic First Amendment principles apply. When the government compels private entities to include speech, it infringes their First Amendment rights. Justice Kagan invoked three important First Amendment precedents establishing this principle.

First, in *Miami Herald v. Tornillo*,[32] the Supreme Court unanimously invalidated a state law that required newspapers to provide space to political candidates who had been attacked in print.[33] The Court stressed that freedom of the press gave the newspaper the right to decide what was included or excluded.[34] Forcing newspapers to publish a reply was deemed to intrude on editorial discretion that is protected by the First Amendment.

Second, in *Pacific Gas & Electric Co. v. Public Utilities Commission of California*,[35] the Court declared unconstitutional a regulation that required private utility companies to include in their billing envelope materials prepared by a public interest group.[36] The regulation sought to provide a more balanced presentation of views on energy issues; the public interest group's statements were to be a counterpoint to the statements by the utility companies. But the Court found that such compelled access violated the First Amendment. Justice Lewis Powell, writing for the Court, said that "[c]ompelled access like that ordered in this case both penalizes the expression of particular points of view and forces speakers to alter their speech to conform with an agenda they do not set."[37]

Third, in *Hurley v. Irish-American Gay, Lesbian, and Bisexual Group of Boston*,[38] the Court held that a private group that organized a St. Patrick's Day parade could exclude a gay, lesbian, and bisexual group from participation.[39] The unanimous decision said that organizing a parade is an inherently expressive activity and that those doing so have a right to exclude messages inimical to their own.[40] The Court explained that compelling the Veterans Council to include the Irish-American Gay, Lesbian, and Bisexual Group "violates the fundamental rule . . . under the First Amendment that a speaker has the autonomy to choose the content of his own message."[41]

After reviewing these cases, Justice Kagan explained their relevance: "First, the First Amendment offers protection when an entity engaging in expressive activity, including compiling and curating others' speech, is directed to accommodate messages it would prefer to exclude. '[T]he editorial function itself is an aspect of speech.' . . . Second, none of that changes just because a compiler includes most items and excludes just a few. . . . Third, the government cannot get its way just by asserting an interest in improving, or better balancing, the marketplace of ideas."[42]

Justice Kagan also defended the importance of content moderation on social media platforms. She said:

> [I]f Texas's law is enforced, the platforms could not—as they in fact do now—disfavor posts because they:
>
> - support Nazi ideology;
> - advocate for terrorism;
> - espouse racism, Islamophobia, or anti-Semitism;
> - glorify rape or other gender-based violence;
> - encourage teenage suicide and self-injury;
> - discourage the use of vaccines;
> - advise phony treatments for diseases;
> - advance false claims of election fraud.[43]

Although Justice Kagan was clear that the Court was not deciding the constitutionality of the Florida and Texas laws, she expressly disagreed with the Fifth Circuit's approach and strongly signaled that these laws are unconstitutional. Justice Barrett wrote a concurring opinion and was even more explicit about this: "[T]he Eleventh Circuit's understanding of the First Amendment's protection of editorial discretion was generally correct; the Fifth Circuit's was not."[44]

Justice Thomas and Justice Alito each wrote opinions concurring in the judgment strongly disagreeing with the Court's discussing the merits and its view of the Fifth Circuit's decision. Justice Thomas wrote: "I cannot agree, however, with the Court's decision to opine on certain applications of those statutes. The Court's discussion is unnecessary to its holding. Moreover, the Court engages in the exact type of analysis that it chastises the Courts of Appeals for performing."[45] Justice Alito's opinion, joined by Justices Thomas and Gorsuch, had an even angrier tone and also made clear that he would likely uphold the Florida and Texas laws.[46] He argued that the technology is unique and cannot be evaluated under traditional First Amendment principles.

The bottom line is that the cases go back to the lower courts to engage in the facial constitutional analysis the Court prescribed. But the constitutionality of state laws prohibiting content moderation is sure to return to the Court soon. And although the Court did not resolve the issue, Justice Kagan's opinion, strongly disapproving of the Fifth Circuit's approach, gives a clear sense of what the Court is likely to decide.

The First Amendment and Trademark Law

The final First Amendment case of the term involved whether a provision of the federal trademark law, the Lanham Act, violates the Constitution. Once more, although the result was unanimous, there were many different opinions, reflecting serious methodological disputes among the justices.

Vidal v. Elster involved an attempt to register a trademark, "Trump too small," which refers to an exchange between Donald Trump and Marco Rubio during a Republican debate in 2016.[47] But the Lanham Act prohibits registration of a trademark that "[c]onsists of or comprises a name . . . identifying a particular living individual except by his written consent."[48] The Supreme Court rejected the constitutional challenge and upheld this provision and its application.

Justice Thomas wrote the opinion for the Court, though in part it was for a majority and in part for a plurality. Justice Thomas said that the Lanham Act provision was a content-based restriction on speech, but strict scrutiny was not required. He based this conclusion on history. He said: "Trademark rights 'ha[ve] been long recognized by the common law and the chancery courts of England and of this country, and by the statutes of some of the States,' and that protection continues today. . . . And, for the duration of that history, the inherently content-based nature of trademark law has never been a cause for constitutional concern. Our country has recognized trademark rights since the founding."[49]

In reading Justice Thomas's opinion, there is the strong sense that he was analyzing the First Amendment in the same manner as he did for the Second Amendment in *New York State Rifle and Pistol Association v. Bruen*: focusing entirely on history and eschewing the traditional levels of scrutiny.[50]

But this approach received significant pushback from other justices. Even Justice Barrett, a self-avowed originalist who had been in the majority in *Bruen*, disagreed that history could provide the answer here. She wrote: "The Court claims that 'history and tradition' settle the constitutionality of the names clause, rendering it unnecessary to adopt a standard for gauging whether a content-based trademark registration restriction abridges the right to free speech. That is wrong twice over. First, the Court's evidence, consisting of loosely related cases from the late-19th and early-20th centuries, does not establish a historical analogue for the names clause. Second, the Court never explains why hunting for historical forebears on a restriction-by-restriction basis is the right way to analyze the constitutional question."[51] She urged a different test and said: "I would adopt a standard, grounded in both trademark law and First Amendment precedent, that reflects the relationship between content-based trademark registration restrictions and free speech. In my view, such restrictions, whether new or old, are permissible so long as they are reasonable in light of the trademark system's purpose of facilitating source identification."[52]

Justice Sotomayor expressed a similar viewpoint. She stressed that there were not federal trademark laws until well into the 20th century and there was not a prohibition on using someone's name or likeness without consent until even later. She rejected shifting to a historical test and said that traditional First Amendment doctrines should be applied. She wrote: "In deciding how to evaluate this kind of challenge, the Court faces two options: Either look only to the history and tradition of the condition, or look to trademark law and settled First Amendment precedent. The first option, which asks whether the history of a particular trademark registration bar plays well with the First Amendment, leads this Court into uncharted territory that neither party requests. The other guides it through well-trodden terrain. I would follow the well-trodden path."[53]

As in *United States v. Rahimi*—a Second Amendment case discussed in Chapter 10—there is significant disagreement among the justices as to whether to follow originalism and, if so, how to apply it. It will be interesting to see in the years ahead whether Justice Thomas's attempt to use originalism under the First Amendment gets more traction, as it did in the Second Amendment area. But the consequences of a purely historical approach to free speech could have startling implications. For example, the government surely could outlaw blasphemous speech, taking the Lord's name in vain, because it was prohibited at the time of the Constitution.[54] Blasphemy laws were well established and continued to have prominent significance in America even into the 20th century.[55]

Actually, following originalism in the area of freedom of speech also would allow the government to impose great restrictions on political speech. Most notably, seditious libel—false criticism of the government and government officials—was not thought to be protected speech. Congress in 1798—with many of the Constitution's drafters and ratifiers participating—adopted the Alien and Sedition Acts of 1798.[56] The laws prohibited the publication of "false, scandalous, and malicious writing or writings against the government of the United States, or either house of the Congress of the United States, or the President of the United States, with intent to defame . . . ; or to bring them . . . into contempt or disrepute; or to excite against them . . . hatred of the good people of the United States, or to stir up sedition within the United States, or to excite any unlawful combinations therein, for opposing or resisting any law of the United States, or any act of the President of the United States."[57]

It is hard to imagine that the current Court would want to uphold such restrictions on political speech, yet if the Court were to take a purely historical approach as it did for the Second Amendment in *Bruen*, it is very difficult to see why such laws would be unconstitutional.

Conclusion

It was a strange year for the First Amendment in the Supreme Court. There were no cases about the religion clauses. The speech cases had the potential for being enormously important but ultimately decided much less than had been anticipated.

Endnotes

1. Knight First Amend. Inst. at Columbia Univ. v. Trump, 928 F.3d 226 (2nd Cir. 2019); Knight First Amend. Inst. at Columbia Univ. v. Trump, 302 F. Supp. 3d 541 (S.D.N.Y. 2018).
2. Lindke v. Freed, 144 S. Ct. 756 (2024).
3. Lindke v. Freed, 37 F.4th 1199 (6th Cir. 2022).
4. *Lindke*, 144 S. Ct. at 766.
5. *Id.* at 766–67.
6. *Id.* at 768.
7. *Id.* at 770.
8. *Id.*
9. Bantam Books, Inc. v. Sullivan, 372 U.S. 58 (1963).
10. Nat'l Rifle Ass'n of Am. v. Vullo, 144 S. Ct. 1316 (2024).
11. *Id.* at 1322.
12. *Id.* at 1328.
13. Murthy v. Missouri, 144 S. Ct. 1972 (2024).
14. *Id.* at 1987–88.
15. *Id.* at 1988.
16. *Id.* at 1997 (Alito, J., dissenting).
17. *Id.* at 1999.
18. *Id.*
19. I discuss these laws, and their desirability, in detail in Alex W. Chemerinsky & Erwin Chemerinsky, *Misguided Federalism: State Regulation of the Internet and Social Media*, 102 N.C. L. Rev. 1 (2023).

20. Fla. Stat. § 504.2041(1)(g).

21. *See* NetChoice v. Att'y Gen., Fla., 34 F.4th 1196, 1232 (11th Cir. 2022) (enjoining all six anticensorship provisions).

22. Fla. Stat. § 106.072(2).

23. *Id.* § 501.2041(2)(j).

24. The Texas law defines "[s]ocial media platform" to include all "Internet website[s] or application[s]" that are "open to the public, allow[] a user to create an account, and enable users to communicate with other users for the primary purpose of posting information, comments, messages or images." Tex. Bus. & Com. Code § 120.001(1). Social media platforms do not include internet service providers, email applications, or entities that consist primarily of non-user-generated content or where chat and comment functions are incidental to the service. *Id.* § 120.001(1)(A)–(C). H.B. 20 only applies to platforms with more than 50 million monthly users in the United States. Tex. Civ. Prac. & Rem. Code § 143A.004(c).

25. Tex. Civ. Prac. & Rem. Code § 143A.002(a).

26. *Id.* § 143A.002(b).

27. NetChoice v. Att'y Gen., Fla., 34 F.4th 1196 (11th Cir. 2022).

28. NetChoice v. Paxton, 49 F.4th 439 (5th Cir. 2022).

29. Moody v. NetChoice, 144 S. Ct. 2383, 2397 (2024).

30. *Id.* at 2397–98.

31. *Id.* at 2399.

32. Miami Herald v. Tornillo, 418 U.S. 241 (1974).

33. *Id. See also* FCC v. League of Women Voters, 468 U.S. 364 (1984) (declaring unconstitutional a federal law that prohibited noncommercial educational stations from editorializing as violating the First Amendment).

34. But see *Red Lion Broadcasting Co. v. FCC*, 395 U.S. 367 (1969), which upheld the fairness doctrine as applied to television and radio. The Court stressed the scarcity of the broadcast spectrum as a basis for allowing the regulation. There is no similar scarcity with regard to the internet and social media; quite the contrary, its core characteristic is its virtually infinite capacity for speech.

35. Pac. Gas & Elec. Co. v. Pub. Utils. Comm'n of Cal., 475 U.S. 1 (1986).

36. *Id.*

37. *Id.* at 9.

38. Hurley v. Irish-Am. Gay, Lesbian & Bisexual Grp. of Bos., 515 U.S. 557 (1995).

39. *Id.*

40. *See id.* at 572.

41. *Id.*

42. Moody v. NetChoice, 144 S. Ct. 2383, 2401–02 (2024).

43. *Id.* at 2405.

44. *Id.* at 2409 (Barrett, J., concurring).

45. *Id.* at 2412 (Thomas, J., concurring).
46. *Id.* at 2422 (Alito, J., concurring).
47. Vidal v. Elster, 144 S. Ct. 1507 (2024).
48. *Id.* at 1512.
49. *Id.* at 1516.
50. *See* N.Y. State Rifle & Pistol Ass'n v. Bruen, 142 S. Ct. 2111 (2022).
51. *Vidal*, 144 S. Ct. at 1524–25 (Barrett, J., concurring).
52. *Id.* at 1525.
53. *Id.* at 1532 (Sotomayor, J., concurring).
54. Phillip I. Blumberg, Repressive Jurisprudence in the Early American Republic: The First Amendment and the Legacy of English Law 323 (2010).
55. *Id.* at 319, 327.
56. Alien and Sedition Acts of July 14, 1798, 1 Stat. 596 (one law was repealed by the Naturalization Law of 1802; the other three were left until they expired).
57. *Id.*

10

Guns

In October Term 2023, the Supreme Court decided two cases concerning firearms. One, *United States v. Rahimi*, involved the Second Amendment and how it should be interpreted.[1] The other, *Garland v. Cargill*, did not raise a constitutional issue but involved the permissibility of a federal regulation prohibiting bump stocks, a device that allows a rifle to fire repeatedly and act like a machine gun.[2]

United States v. Rahimi and the Second Amendment

The Second Amendment says, "A well regulated Militia, being necessary to the security of a free State, the right of the people to keep and bear Arms, shall not be infringed." From 1791 until 2008, the Supreme Court never once declared unconstitutional any law—federal, state, or local—as violating the Second Amendment. In the handful of cases about the provision, the Court said that it was just about a right to have guns for militia service.[3]

In June 2008, in *District of Columbia v. Heller*, the Court for the first time declared a gun regulation unconstitutional and struck down a 32-year-old District of Columbia ordinance that prohibited ownership or possession of handguns.[4] The decision was ideologically split, 5–4, with

Justice Antonin Scalia writing the opinion for the Court. Justice Scalia traced the history of gun rights in England and the states prior to the ratification of the Constitution. He said: "We therefore believe that the most likely reading of all four of these pre-Second Amendment state constitutional provisions is that they secured an individual right to bear arms for defensive purposes."[5] Justice Scalia then looked at the post-ratification commentary, the pre–Civil War cases, and the post–Civil War legislation and cases and said that all of these confirm that the Second Amendment was not meant to be limited to a right to have firearms for militia service.

The Court held that the Second Amendment protects a right to have guns in the home for the sake of security. The Court did not prescribe a level of scrutiny, but it made clear that the Second Amendment is not absolute. The Court said that the government can regulate who has guns, such as keeping those with a felony conviction or history of serious mental illness from having guns. Also, the government can limit where people have guns, such as prohibiting them near schools or public places. And the government can prevent people from having especially dangerous weapons.[6]

Two years later, in *McDonald v. City of Chicago* (2010), the Supreme Court held, again 5–4, that the Second Amendment applies to state and local governments.[7] Because the District of Columbia is a part of the federal government, it took a separate decision to hold that the Second Amendment is incorporated into the due process clause of the 14th Amendment and applies to state and local governments.

The Court did not return to the scope of the Second Amendment until 2022 in *New York State Rifle and Pistol Association v. Bruen*.[8] A New York law, initially adopted in 1911, prohibited having weapons in public without a permit. If a person wanted to carry a firearm outside the home or place of business for self-defense, the applicant had to obtain an unrestricted license to "have and carry" a concealed "pistol or revolver."[9] To secure that license, the applicant must prove that "proper cause exists" to issue it.[10] This required that the individual show a safety need for having the gun outside the home.

In a 6–3 decision, with the majority opinion written by Justice Clarence Thomas, the Court declared the New York law unconstitutional. The Court held that state laws are unconstitutional if they restrict having concealed weapons to those who show cause. The Court said that a gun regulation is constitutionally permissible *only* if it was historically allowed. The Court declared: "To justify its regulation, the government may not simply posit that the regulation promotes an important interest. Rather, the government must demonstrate that the regulation is consistent with this Nation's historical tradition of firearm regulation. Only if a firearm regulation is consistent with this Nation's historical tradition may a court conclude that the individual's conduct falls outside the Second Amendment's 'unqualified command.'"[11]

The Court expressly rejected any balancing of the government's interests in regulating guns with a claim of Second Amendment rights. Justice Thomas wrote, "The Second Amendment 'is the *very product* of an interest balancing by the people,' and *it 'surely elevates above all other interests* the right of law-abiding, responsible citizens to use arms' for self-defense."[12] The Court said that it was rejecting any analysis of means and ends, such as whether the government regulation serves a compelling interest and whether it is necessary to achieve the goal. This is a different approach than the Court has taken for other rights or for equal protection, where it has applied the levels of scrutiny. For fundamental rights under due process or even for racial discrimination under equal protection, the government can prevail if it meets strict scrutiny. But for the Second Amendment the Court said it is entirely a question of whether the gun regulation is of a type that was historically permitted.

Since *Bruen*, not surprisingly, there have been hundreds of challenges to gun regulations of all types. There has been great confusion in the lower courts over how to apply the historical test prescribed by *Bruen. United States v. Rahimi* is important because it is the first time since *Bruen* that the Court has addressed the meaning of the Second Amendment. Interestingly, the decision in *Rahimi* was 8–1, but there were seven different opinions. Mostly they were about how to apply the *Bruen* test and more generally about how to engage in originalist analysis. Quite importantly, the Court in *Rahimi* used and clarified *Bruen*'s historical approach; it did not back away from the focus on history or imply a use of the levels of scrutiny.

Rahimi involves a federal statute, 18 U.S.C. § 922(g)(8), that makes it a federal crime for a person under a restraining order in a domestic violence case to have a firearm. Zackey Rahimi physically abused his girlfriend in a parking lot and fired his gun when he saw a bystander. Although Rahimi called her and threated to shoot her if she reported the incident, she went to court and got a restraining order preventing Rahimi from having contact with her or her family for two years. The court, in issuing the restraining order, suspended Rahimi's gun license and informed him of the federal law that kept him from having a gun during the time of the restraining order.

Rahimi was subsequently the suspect in many other shootings, and the police obtained a warrant to search his home. They found a large number of weapons there, as well as a copy of the judge's order keeping him from having guns. Rahimi was charged with violating § 922(g). In the federal district court, Rahimi unsuccessfully challenged the constitutionality of the law. He pled guilty, with the condition that he could appeal. A sentence of 73 months in prison was imposed.

The U.S. Court of Appeals for the Fifth Circuit ruled in Rahimi's favor.[13] It applied the test from *Bruen* and said that the question is whether § 922(g) is the type of restriction that existed historically. The Fifth Circuit focused on laws in 1791 when the Second Amendment was adopted and concluded that there were not laws then that made it a crime for those under a restraining order in a domestic violence case to have guns. The court said there is "no tradition—from 1791 or 1866—of prohibiting gun possession . . . for people . . . subject to civil protective orders."[14] The court said that this made § 922(g) unconstitutional.

The Supreme Court, in an 8–1 decision, reversed and upheld the federal statute. It is worth noting that the context of the case is very different from *Heller*, *McDonald*, and *Bruen*. Unlike those cases, *Rahimi* arose in the context of a criminal prosecution and a criminal defendant's challenge to a gun regulation.

Chief Justice Roberts wrote the opinion for the Court and declared: "When a restraining order contains a finding that an individual poses a credible threat to the physical safety of an intimate partner, that individual may—consistent with the Second Amendment—be banned from possessing firearms while the order is in effect. Since the founding, our Nation's firearm laws have included provisions preventing individuals who threaten physical harm to others from misusing firearms. As applied to the facts of this case, Section 922(g)(8) fits comfortably within this tradition."[15]

Significantly, Chief Justice Roberts's majority opinion explicitly used the approach from *Bruen*. Nowhere in the majority opinion does the Court discuss the justification for the statute: protecting victims of domestic violence, especially women. The contemporary need for the law was never mentioned by the Court. Instead, the Court clarified the methodology from *Bruen* and stated: "[S]ome courts have misunderstood the methodology of our recent Second Amendment cases. These precedents were not meant to suggest a law trapped in amber."[16]

The Court then prescribed the approach that lower courts are to take in determining the constitutionality of gun laws. It wrote: "Even when a law regulates arms-bearing for a permissible reason, though, it may not be compatible with the right if it does so to an extent beyond what was done at the founding. And when a challenged regulation does not precisely match its historical precursors, 'it still may be analogous enough to pass constitutional muster.' The law must comport with the principles underlying the Second Amendment, but it need not be a 'dead ringer' or a 'historical twin.'"[17] The Court said that § 922(g)(8) is constitutional because history supports that "when an individual poses a clear threat of physical violence to another, the threatening individual may be disarmed."[18]

Five justices—Sotomayor, Gorsuch, Kavanaugh, Barrett, and Jackson—wrote concurring opinions. They largely argued over whether originalism should be used and, if so, how to apply it. Justice Sotomayor, joined by Justice Kagan, said she continued to disagree with *Bruen*'s approach, but if it is to be used, there does not have to be an identical historical "match" for a law in order for it to be a constitutional regulation of guns.[19] She said that "[e]ven under *Bruen*, this is an easy case" because of the history of denying guns to individuals who have been deemed dangerous.[20] She said that the key question is whether the gun regulation is consistent with the "principles" underlying the Second Amendment.[21]

Justice Gorsuch wrote a concurring opinion taking a quite different approach. He was emphatic that the meaning of a constitutional provision is fixed when it was adopted and can change only through the amendment process. He wrote: "[W]e seek to honor the fact that the Second Amendment 'codified a *pre-existing* right' belonging to the American people, one that carries the same 'scope' today that it was 'understood to have when the people adopted' it. . . . We have no authority to question that judgment."[22] Unlike Chief Justice Roberts, he does see the meaning of the Constitution frozen in amber. He stated: "As judges charged with respecting the people's directions in the Constitution—directions that are 'trapped in amber,' . . . —our only lawful role is to apply them in the cases that come before us. Developments in the world may change, facts on the ground may evolve, and new laws may invite new challenges, but the Constitution the people adopted remains our enduring guide. If changes are to be made to the Constitution's directions, they must be made by the American people."[23] He decided to uphold the law because there were sufficiently similar limits on possessing firearms in 1791.

Justice Kavanaugh wrote a concurring opinion that strongly supported originalism but would expand it to including consideration of post-ratification history of a provision. He wrote: "[T]he Court interprets and applies the Constitution by examining text, pre-ratification and post-ratification history, and precedent."[24] Justice Kavanaugh contrasted two ways of interpreting the Constitution: one that focuses on history and the other that looks at policy. He said that justices are like "umpires," and citing to the works of originalists Robert Bork and Antonin Scalia, Justice Kavanaugh said: "And in a constitutional system that counts on an independent Judiciary, judges must act like umpires. To be an umpire, the judge 'must stick close to the text and the history, and their fair implications,' because there 'is no principled way' for a neutral judge 'to prefer any claimed human value to any other.'"[25] Justice Kavanaugh rejected balancing, including the use of levels of scrutiny, as justices making policy, not following history. This is Justice Kavanaugh's most emphatic embracing of originalism since coming on the Court.

Justice Barrett also wrote a concurring opinion embracing originalism, but her version was more flexible and like that of the majority opinion.[26] She wrote: "To be *consistent* with historical limits, a challenged regulation need not be an updated model of a historical counterpart. Besides, imposing a test that demands overly specific analogues has serious problems. To name two: It forces 21st-century regulations to follow late-18th-century policy choices, giving us 'a law trapped in amber.' And it assumes that founding-era legislatures maximally exercised their power to regulate, thereby adopting a 'use it or lose it' view of legislative authority."[27] She said that she joined the majority opinion because it used the right level of generality in defining the scope of the Second Amendment.

Justice Jackson also wrote a concurring opinion, but she disagreed with *Bruen* and using originalism to determine the meaning of the Second Amendment.[28] She lamented the confusion the *Bruen* approach was causing in the lower courts and said that *Rahimi* did little to solve the problem.

Only Justice Thomas, the author of the majority opinion in *Bruen*, dissented.[29] Like the Fifth Circuit, Justice Thomas would have invalidated the federal statute because there were not similar statutes in 1791. He wrote: "A firearm regulation that falls within the Second Amendment's plain text is unconstitutional unless it is consistent with the Nation's historical tradition of firearm regulation. Not a single historical regulation justifies the statute at issue."[30]

The case is significant in many ways. Upholding this law is, in itself, quite important. Keeping those under restraining orders in domestic violence cases from having guns will save many lives, especially women's lives. The Educational Fund to Stop Gun Violence reports that "[a] woman is five times more likely to be murdered when her abuser has access to a gun."[31]

The Court's decision is significant, too, in making it much more likely that many other gun regulations will be allowed. Chief Justice Roberts's majority opinion rejects the view that gun regulations are constitutional only if they are of a type that existed in 1791. For example, there is a federal law, and laws in almost every state, that prohibits convicted felons from having guns.[32] There have been hundreds of challenges to these laws in the last two years, and there is a split among the lower courts as to whether they violate the Second Amendment.[33] The Court's ruling provides a strong basis for upholding these laws, as the justices made clear that the government can keep those who have been found by a court to be a threat to others from having guns.

But the case still leaves confusion as to how courts are to apply the historical test from *Bruen*. A central problem with originalism is determining what is the appropriate level of abstraction with which to look at the history.[34] If the Court says that a constitutional provision must mean exactly what it meant when it was adopted, this will lead to clearly unacceptable results. For example, if that were to be the standard, *Brown v. Board of Education* was wrongly decided because the same Congress that ratified the 14th Amendment also segregated the District of Columbia public schools and clearly did not have in mind that the assurance of equal protection would outlaw segregation.[35] But that is the logic that the Fifth Circuit deployed in striking down the federal law in *Rahimi*; no laws existed to prohibit those under restraining orders in domestic violence cases from having guns in 1791, so none can exist today. That is the basis for Justice Thomas's dissent in *Rahimi*.

An alternative way of approaching originalism is to look more generally at history in interpreting a constitutional provision, not limiting its meaning to the specific understandings of the time, but instead focusing on the underlying principles behind a provision. This was what the Supreme Court did in its review of the Fifth Circuit's *Rahimi* decision. Chief Justice Roberts in his majority opinion emphasized that courts considering the constitutionality of restrictions on gun rights must determine "whether the new law is 'relevantly similar' to laws that our tradition is understood to permit, applying faithfully the balance struck by the founding generation to modern circumstances."[36] The Court said that historical examples abound of dangerous people being kept from having guns, and thus the federal law at question in *Rahimi* is justified.

The problem with this approach for originalists is that originalism then loses the constraint on judging that originalism seeks to promise. When traditions at a more general level of abstraction can be considered, then originalism becomes indeterminate; almost any result can be justified, and originalism becomes indistinguishable from nonoriginalism. Thus, in *Rahimi* the Court confronted a central problem of originalism: look narrowly at the understandings of 1791 and come to an unacceptable conclusion, or look more generally at history and allow the justices to justify whatever result they want.

And, of course, those who reject originalism say that the understandings of 1791 should not limit the Constitution's meaning today. Tragically, in 1791, there were not laws or restraining orders about domestic violence. The liberal justices—Sotomayor, Kagan, and Jackson—argued that § 922(g)(8) is constitutional because it serves the compelling interest of saving lives.

There likely will be many Supreme Court cases in the years ahead about the Second Amendment and issues about who can be kept from having guns, what type of weapons can be prohibited, and what restrictions can be imposed as to where people can have guns.

Garland v. Cargill

In *Garland v. Cargill*, the Court, in a 6–3 decision split along ideological lines, invalidated a rule adopted by the Bureau of Alcohol, Tobacco, Firearms, and Explosives (ATF) that prohibited a device, bump stocks, that effectively turns rifles into machine guns.[37] Although the case involved the interpretation of a federal law and not the Second Amendment, the division among the justices reflected the familiar division between conservatives and liberals over gun rights as opposed to gun regulation.

Federal statutes adopted in 1934 and 1968 prohibit people from having machine guns.[38] Congress did so because machine guns have the capacity to fire many bullets quickly and thus cause enormous harm. The law defines a machine gun as one that automatically fires "more than one shot, without manual reloading, by a single function of the trigger."[39] In other words, a machine gun allows the shooter to fire multiple times, or even continuously, by pressing the trigger only once. By contrast, with a semiautomatic firearm the shooter must release and reengage the trigger to fire each shot.

A bump stock is a device that allows a semiautomatic gun to repeatedly fire. It replaces the rifle's standard stock, which is the part held against the shoulder. It allows a weapon to fire at nearly the rate of a machine gun; a rifle equipped with a bump stock can fire at a rate between 400 and 800 rounds per minute.[40]

In 2017, a gunman in Las Vegas fired into a crowd attending a music festival, killing 58 people and wounding over 500 more. The gunman's weapons had bump stocks, which allowed him to fire hundreds of rounds in a matter of minutes.

The tragedy in Las Vegas caused the ATF to change its position and adopt a rule that deemed bump stocks to be prohibited by the federal statute outlawing machine guns. It is worth noting that the new rule was adopted by the conservative Trump administration and followed even the National Rifle Association's calling for restrictions on bump stocks. The rule ordered owners of bump stocks to destroy them or surrender them to ATF within 90 days. Failure to do so was a federal crime.

The government defended the ATF rule outlawing bump stocks, arguing that they serve no purpose other than to turn semiautomatic weapons effectively into machine guns. All of the reasons that Congress outlawed machine guns in 1934 apply to bump stocks. The government contended that bump stocks facilitate the firing of a large number of bullets—and facilitate the shooting of a large number of people—in a short amount of time. As a matter of interpreting the federal law, it makes sense to treat bump stocks as machine guns. As Justice Sonia Sotomayor said in her dissent, "When I see a bird that walks like duck, swims like a duck, and quacks like a duck, I call that bird a duck."[41]

But the Court, in a majority opinion written by Justice Thomas, called bump stocks different from machine guns and said that therefore the ATF lacked the authority to adopt its rule. The Court focused on the language of the federal statute and said that a machine gun requires only one firing of the trigger, whereas even a "semiautomatic rifle equipped with a bump stock does not fire more than one shot 'by a single function of the trigger.'"[42] The majority said that "[a]ll that a bump stock does is accelerate the rate of fire by causing these distinct 'function[s]' of the trigger to occur in rapid succession."[43]

Justice Sotomayor wrote for the dissent and objected that the Court also failed to follow the principle that statutes should be interpreted to fulfill their purpose. She wrote that a "bump-stock-equipped semiautomatic rifle fires 'automatically more than one shot, without manual reloading, by a single function of the trigger.'"[44] That fits within the definition of a machine gun under the federal statute.

Both Justice Thomas's majority opinion and Justice Sotomayor's dissent include detailed descriptions of how bump stocks work. Both agree, and it is unassailable, that bump stocks allow a semiautomatic weapon to perform exactly as a machine gun. And it also is undeniable that such weapons can kill a large number of people in a short amount of time.

The Court's 6–3 ruling, split along ideological lines, should be no surprise. *Heller*, *McDonald*, and *Bruen* also were similarly divided. For whatever reasons, for decades it has been that conservatives favor gun rights and liberals favor gun regulations. *Garland v. Cargill* reflects that split.

Because this case does not involve the Second Amendment, Congress could adopt a law prohibiting bump stocks. The gun lobby has so far prevented this from happening. But it is possible in the future.

Endnotes

1. United States v. Rahimi, 144 S. Ct. 1889 (2024).
2. Garland v. Cargill, 602 U.S. 406 (2024).
3. *See, e.g.*, United States v. Miller, 307 U.S. 174 (1939); Presser v. Illinois, 116 U.S. 252 (1886); United States v. Cruikshank, 92 U.S. 542 (1875).
4. Dist. of Columbia v. Heller, 554 U.S. 570 (2008).
5. *Id.* at 602.
6. *Id.* at 626–27.
7. McDonald v. City of Chi., 561 U.S. 742 (2010).
8. N.Y. State Rifle & Pistol Ass'n v. Bruen, 597 U.S. 1 (2022).
9. *Id.* at 11.
10. *Id.*
11. *Id.* at 17 (quoting Konigsberg v. State Bar of Cal., 366 U.S. 36, 50 n.10 (1961)).
12. *Id.* at 2–3 (emphasis added) (quoting Dist. of Columbia v. Heller, 554 U.S. 570, 635 (2008)).
13. United States v. Rahimi, 61 F.4th 443 (5th Cir. 2023).
14. *Id.* at 460 n.11.
15. United States v. Rahimi, 144 S. Ct. at 1896-97.
16. *Id.* at 1897.
17. *Id.* at 1898 (citations omitted).
18. *Id.* at 1901.
19. *Id.* at 1904 (Sotomayor, J., concurring).
20. *Id.*
21. *Id.*

22. *Id.* at 1907-08 (Gorsuch, J. concurring) (quoting Dist. of Columbia v. Heller, 554 U.S. 570, 634–35 (2008)).

23. *Id.* at 1908.

24. *Id.* at 1910 (Kavanaugh, J., concurring).

25. *Id.* at 1912 (citations omitted).

26. *Id.* at 1924 (Barrett, J., dissenting).

27. *Id.* at 1925.

28. *Id.* at 1926 (Jackson, J., concurring).

29. *Id.* at 1930 (Thomas, J., dissenting).

30. *Id.*

31. Educ. Fund to Stop Gun Violence, *Domestic Violence and Firearms* (July 2020), https://efsgv.org/learn/type-of-gun-violence/domestic-violence-and-firearms/.

32. *See, e.g.*, 18 U.S.C. § 922(g)(1); CAL. PENAL CODE § 29800; FLA. STAT. § 790.23; N.Y. PENAL LAW § 400.00; TEX. PENAL CODE § 46.04.

33. *Compare* United States v. Duarte, 101 F.4th 657 (9th Cir. 2024); Range v. Att'y Gen., 69 F.4th 96 (3d Cir. 2023) (vacated and remanded by *Rahimi* on July 2, 2024) (holding unconstitutional prohibitions on felons possessing firearms) *with* United States v. Gay, 98 F.4th 843 (7th Cir. 2024); United States v. Jackson, 69 F.4th 495 (8th Cir. 2023) (vacated and remanded by *Rahimi* on July 2, 2024); Vincent v. Garland, 80 F.4th 1197 (10th Cir. 2023) (vacated and remanded by *Rahimi* on July 2, 2024); United States v. Dubois, 94 F.4th 1284 (11th Cir. 2024) (holding constitutional prohibitions on felons possessing firearms).

34. I explain this point in ERWIN CHEMERINSKY, WORSE THAN NOTHING: THE DANGEROUS FALLACY OF ORIGINALISM 182 (2022).

35. Brown v. Bd. of Educ., 347 U.S. 483 (1954); *see* CHEMERINSKY, *supra* note 34, at 94–102.

36. United States v. Rahimi, 144 S. Ct. at 1898 (quoting N.Y. State Rifle & Pistol Ass'n v. Bruen, 597 U.S. 1, 29 (2022)).

37. Garland v. Cargill, 602 U.S. 406, 406 (2024).

38. 26 U.S.C. § 5845(b); 18 U.S.C. § 922(o).

39. 26 U.S.C. § 5845(b).

40. *Garland*, 602 U.S. at 434 (Sotomayor, J., dissenting).

41. *Id.* at 430.

42. *Id.* at 415.

43. *Id.*

44. *Id.* at 430 (Sotomayor, J., dissenting).

11

Immigration Law

The Supreme Court's decision in *Department of State v. Munoz* was the most important immigration law decision of the term and also is significant for its approach to due process.[1] The Court held that a citizen does not have a fundamental liberty interest in her noncitizen spouse being admitted to the country.

In 2010, Sandra Muñoz, an American citizen, married Luis Asencio-Cordero, a citizen of El Salvador. The couple sought to obtain an immigrant visa for Asencio-Cordero so that they could live together in the United States. Asencio-Cordero submitted an application for a visa at the U.S. consulate in San Salvador. A consular officer denied his application though gave no reason for this decision. Because Asencio-Cordero is a noncitizen, he has no constitutional right to enter the United States and could not challenge the denial of his visa.

Muñoz, as a citizen, filed a challenge to the consular officer's decision. As the Supreme Court explained, her argument was: "The right to live with her noncitizen spouse in the United States is implicit in the 'liberty' protected by the Fifth Amendment; the denial of her husband's visa deprived her of this interest, thereby triggering her right to due process; the consular officer violated her right to due process by declining to disclose the basis for finding Asencio-Cordero inadmissible; and this, in turn, enables judicial review, even though visa denials are ordinarily unreviewable by courts."[2]

After Muñoz filed suit in the federal district court, she learned the basis for the consular officer's decision: he believed that Asencio-Cordero is affiliated with MS-13, a criminal gang. The consular officer came to this conclusion even though Asencio-Cordero had no criminal record; the conclusion was based on Asencio-Cordero's tattoos.

The U.S. Court of Appeals for the Ninth Circuit ruled in favor of Muñoz. It held that Muñoz, as a citizen, had a constitutionally protected liberty interest in her husband's visa application. It said that due process required the State Department to give Muñoz a "facially legitimate and bona fide reason" for denying her husband's visa.[3]

The U.S. Supreme Court, in a 6–3 decision, reversed the Ninth Circuit and ruled against Muñoz. Justice Barrett wrote the opinion for the Court, which was joined by Chief Justice Roberts and Justices Thomas, Alito, and Kavanaugh. Justice Gorsuch concurred in the judgment. Justice Sotomayor wrote a strong dissent, joined by Justices Kagan and Jackson.

Justice Barrett began the majority opinion by invoking the doctrine of consular nonreviewability. She said that this means that "[t]he Immigration and Nationality Act (INA) does not authorize judicial review of a consular officer's denial of a visa; thus, as a rule, the federal courts cannot review those decisions."[4]

Muñoz's argument was that as a U.S. citizen she could obtain judicial review based on an infringement of the constitutional right to live with her spouse in her country of citizenship. She contended that she was denied fair procedures, which are required by the due process clause.

The Supreme Court, though, rejected this argument, holding that "a citizen does not have a fundamental liberty interest in her noncitizen spouse being admitted to the country."[5] Although this was a case about procedural due process—what notice and procedures Muñoz is entitled to—the Court used its substantive due process analysis for determining whether there is a liberty interest. As the Court did two years earlier in *Dobbs v. Jackson Women's Health Organization*[6] in overruling *Roe v. Wade*,[7] it used the test from *Washington v. Glucksberg*[8] and stated that the Court "exercise[s] the utmost care whenever we are asked to break new ground in this field. To that end, *Glucksberg*'s two-step inquiry disciplines the substantive due process analysis. First, it insists on a 'careful description of the asserted fundamental liberty interest.' Second, it stresses that 'the Due Process Clause specially protects' only 'those fundamental rights and liberties which are, objectively, deeply rooted in this Nation's history and tradition.'"[9]

The Court ruled that Muñoz failed to show a fundamental liberty interest under this test. The Court explained that Muñoz could not demonstrate "that the right to bring a noncitizen spouse to the United States is 'deeply rooted in this Nation's history and tradition.' On the contrary, the through line of history is recognition of the Government's sovereign authority to set the terms governing the admission and exclusion of noncitizens. And Muñoz points to no subsidiary tradition that curbs this authority in the case of noncitizen spouses."[10]

The Court also said that allowing Muñoz's claim to a "procedural due process right in *someone else's* legal proceeding" would lead to undesirable consequences: "Could a wife challenge her husband's assignment to a remote prison or to an overseas military deployment, even though prisoners and service members themselves cannot bring such challenges? Could a citizen assert procedural rights in the removal proceeding of her spouse?"[11]

Justice Sotomayor wrote a vehement dissent. She argued that "there is no question that excluding a citizen's spouse burdens her right to marriage, and that burden requires the Government to provide at least a factual basis for its decision."[12] Muñoz's fundamental right to marry included a right to be with her husband in the United States, and that liberty interest required procedural due process. Justice Sotomayor explained: "The constitutional right to marriage is not so flimsy. The Government cannot banish a U.S. citizen's spouse and give only a bare statutory citation as an excuse. By denying Muñoz the right to a factual basis for her husband's exclusion, the majority departs from longstanding precedent and gravely undervalues the right to marriage in the immigration context."[13]

Justice Sotomayor concluded by declaring, "Muñoz may be able to live with her husband in El Salvador, but it will mean raising her U. S.-citizen child outside the United States. Others will be less fortunate. The burden will fall most heavily on same-sex couples and others who lack the ability, for legal or financial reasons, to make a home in the noncitizen spouse's country of origin. For those couples, this Court's vision of marriage as the 'assurance that while both still live there will be someone to care for the other' rings hollow."[14]

The case is important on many levels. In the immigration context, it strongly reaffirms the principle of consular nonreviewability and resolves an issue that the Supreme Court left open in *Kerry v. Din*.[15] In terms of due process, it is notable that the Court used its test under substantive due process for determining whether there is a liberty interest for purposes of procedural due process. And the Court narrowly construed the right to marry, indicating that keeping spouses from living together did not infringe this right.

Endnotes

1. Dep't of State v. Muñoz, 144 S. Ct. 1812 (2024). I should disclose that I was co-counsel for the respondent, Muñoz, in the U.S. Supreme Court.
2. *Id.* at 1817.
3. Muñoz v. Dep't of State, 50 F.4th 906, 916 (2022).
4. *Dep't of State*, 144 S. Ct. at 1820.
5. *Id.* at 1821.
6. Dobbs v. Jackson Women's Health Org., 142 S. Ct. 2228 (2022).
7. Roe v. Wade, 410 U.S. 113 (1973).
8. Washington v. Glucksberg, 521 U.S. 702 (1997).
9. *Dep't of State*, 144 S. Ct. at 1822.
10. *Id.* at 1822–23.
11. *Id.* at 1826.
12. *Id.* at 1829 (Sotomayor, J., dissenting).
13. *Id.* at 1833.
14. *Id.* at 1840.
15. Kerry v. Din, 576 U.S. 86 (2015).

12

Donald Trump in the Supreme Court

The Court decided two very important cases that involved Donald Trump as a litigant. In *Trump v. Anderson*, the Supreme Court unanimously reversed the Colorado Supreme Court and held that a state court did not have the authority to preclude Trump from running for president under Section 3 of the 14th Amendment.[1] In *Trump v. United States*, the Court broadly defined the scope of a president's (or former president's) absolute immunity for criminal prosecution.[2]

Both cases certainly matter for Donald Trump, and each is unquestionably a victory for him. Each, though, has far greater significance for our democracy. In each, the Court addressed a constitutional question that it had never before decided. In each, and especially in *Trump v. United States*, there is great disagreement among the justices.

Trump v. Anderson

Section 3 of the 14th Amendment provides: "No person shall be a Senator or Representative in Congress, or elector of President and Vice-President, or hold any office, civil or military, under the United States, or under any

State, who, having previously taken an oath, as a member of Congress, or as an officer of the United States . . . to support the Constitution of the United States, shall have engaged in insurrection or rebellion against the same, or given aid or comfort to the enemies thereof. But Congress may by a vote of two-thirds of each House, remove such disability."

A lawsuit was brought in Colorado state court arguing that Donald Trump was disqualified from being president under Section 3 of the 14th Amendment because of his role in the January 6 insurrection. After a five-day trial, the state trial court found that former President Trump had "engaged in insurrection" within the meaning of Section 3.[3] But the Colorado trial court held that Section 3 did not apply because the presidency, which Section 3 does not mention by name, is not an "office . . . under the United States" and the president is not an "officer of the United States" within the meaning of that provision.

The Colorado Supreme Court, in a 4–3 decision, concluded that for purposes of Section 3, the presidency is an office of the United States and the president is an officer of the United States.[4] The Colorado Supreme Court accordingly ordered its secretary of state not to "list President Trump's name on the 2024 presidential primary ballot" or "count any write-in votes cast for him."[5]

Lest this be dismissed as partisan, prominent conservatives such as law professors and Federalist Society members William Baude and Michael Paulsen[6] and former federal court of appeals judge Michael Luttig came to the same conclusion.[7] Professors Baude and Paulsen, in a lengthy law review article, concluded that Section 3 precluded Trump from running for or being elected president.

The U.S. Supreme Court unanimously reversed the Colorado Supreme Court and held that a state could not enforce Section 3 of the 14th Amendment. It was a per curiam opinion—an opinion of the Court. Justice Barrett concurred in part and concurred in the judgment in part. Justices Sotomayor, Kagan, and Jackson concurred in the judgment, but the tone was more like a dissent.

The Court concluded that "responsibility for enforcing Section 3 against federal officeholders and candidates rests with Congress and not the States."[8] The Court gave two reasons for its conclusion. First, it said that it was not for states to enforce Section 3 of the 14th Amendment.

The Court stated: "We conclude that States may disqualify persons holding or attempting to hold *state* office. But States have no power under the Constitution to enforce Section 3 with respect to federal offices, especially the Presidency."[9] The Court said that "nothing in the Constitution delegates to the States any power to enforce Section 3 against federal officeholders and candidates."[10] The Court said that it is for Congress, using its power under Section 5 of the 14th Amendment, to enforce Section 3's disqualifications.

The Court raised the concern that varying states would come to differing conclusions as to whether a candidate could run for president. It stated: "But state-by-state resolution of the question whether Section 3 bars a particular candidate for President from serving would be quite unlikely to yield a uniform answer consistent with the basic principle that 'the President . . . represent[s] *all* the voters in the Nation.'"[11] The Court said that the "result could well be that a single candidate would be declared ineligible in some States, but not others, based on the same conduct (and perhaps even the same factual record)."[12]

Second, the Court said that there must be federal legislation to enforce Section 3 of the 14th Amendment. The Court said that Congress must use its powers under Section 5 of that amendment to enact laws to enforce Section 3. It said, "Neither we nor the respondents are aware of any other legislation by Congress to enforce Section 3."[13] Without such legislation, the Court indicated that the judiciary was powerless to enforce it.

Justices Sotomayor, Kagan, and Jackson concurred in the judgment and said that the Court should have relied just on the former argument and not have addressed the latter and required a federal statute to enforce Section 3. They said the former was sufficient for the decision and that it was wrong to go further than that. They stated: "The majority announces that a disqualification for insurrection can occur only when Congress enacts a particular kind of legislation pursuant to Section 5 of the Fourteenth Amendment. In doing so, the majority shuts the door on other potential means of federal enforcement. We cannot join an opinion that decides momentous and difficult issues unnecessarily, and we therefore concur only in the judgment."[14]

These justices disagreed that it should take specific federal legislation to enforce Section 3 of the 14th Amendment. They accused the majority of "attempt[ing] to insulate all alleged insurrectionists from future challenges to their holding federal office."[15] They concluded their opinion: "[T]he majority goes beyond the necessities of this case to limit how Section 3 can bar an oathbreaking insurrectionist from becoming President. Although we agree that Colorado cannot enforce Section 3, we protest the majority's effort to use this case to define the limits of federal enforcement of that provision."[16]

Justice Barrett concurred in part and concurred in the judgment in part. She agreed with Justices Sotomayor, Kagan, and Jackson that the Court should have decided the case just based on the states' lack of power to enforce Section 3. She, too, would not have opined on whether federal legislation is required to enforce that provision. But interestingly, she then went on to chastise Justices Sotomayor, Kagan, and Jackson for their opinion. Justice Barrett wrote: "In my judgment, this is not the time to amplify disagreement with stridency. The Court has settled a politically charged issue in the volatile season of a Presidential election. Particularly in this circumstance, writings on the Court should turn the national temperature down, not up."[17]

Although the Court was unanimous as to the result, questions can be raised as to its reasoning. First, why can't state courts enforce Section 3 of the 14th Amendment? State courts constantly enforce Section 1 of that amendment, so why not Section 3? The Bill of Rights is applied to the states through the due process clause of the 14th Amendment. Literally every day, state courts hearing criminal cases enforce provisions such as the Fourth Amendment's limits on police search and seizures and the Sixth Amendment's requirements during a criminal trial. If a state adopted an unconstitutional law restricting voting, surely state courts could enjoin it. No one ever has questioned the authority of states and state courts to enforce the requirements and prohibitions of the 14th Amendment.

The Court was concerned about individual states making the determination of who can run for president of the United States. But any such determination by a state court is reviewable in the U.S. Supreme Court. Ultimately, it would be for the Supreme Court to decide, for the entire country, if the requirements of Section 3 are met. If a state court disqualifies someone from running for president, as the Colorado Supreme

Court did, the U.S. Supreme Court would review that holding and make a determination for the nation. There would be no risk of states coming to different conclusions.

Second, why should legislation be required to enforce Section 3, any more than for any other constitutional provision? The Constitution is meant to limit the government and should not require congressional action in order to be enforced. In fact, in 1883, in the *Civil Rights Cases*, the Supreme Court declared that the 14th Amendment is "undoubtedly self-executing without any ancillary legislation, so far as its terms are applicable to any existing state of circumstances."[18]

There are other constitutional provisions that limit who can be president. Article II of the Constitution says that the president must be at least 35 years old, a natural-born citizen, and at least 14 years a resident of the United States. A president cannot serve more than two terms. Would these require a federal statute in order for a court to enforce them? Section 3 of the 14th Amendment is another limitation. Why isn't it the role of the courts to enforce all of these constitutional provisions limiting who can be president of the United States?

The immediate effect of *Trump v. Anderson* is that Donald Trump cannot be disqualified from running or holding office based on his conduct related to the insurrection on January 6. The larger implications are to make it very difficult to enforce Section 3 in the future.

Trump v. United States

No case during October Term 2023 received more attention or was more divisive on the Supreme Court than *Trump v. United States*.[19] The issue was whether and to what extent Donald Trump had immunity from criminal prosecution for actions taken to allegedly undermine the outcome of the 2020 presidential election.

Jack Smith, the special counsel, sought an indictment, and a federal grand jury indicted Donald Trump on four counts for conduct that occurred while he was president and that was intended to keep him in office and to deny the presidency to Joe Biden. The indictment said that Trump "used knowingly false claims of election fraud to get state legislators and election officials to . . . change electoral votes for [Trump's] opponent, Joseph R. Biden, Jr., to electoral votes for [Trump]." It also said that Trump and his co-conspirators "organized fraudulent slates of electors in seven targeted states" and "caused these fraudulent electors to transmit their false certificates to the Vice President and other government officials to be counted at the certification proceeding on January 6." Third, Trump and his co-conspirators attempted to use the Justice Department "to conduct sham election crime investigations and to send a letter to the targeted states that falsely claimed that the Justice Department had identified significant concerns that may have impacted the election outcome." Fourth, Trump and his co-conspirators attempted to persuade "the Vice President to use his ceremonial role at the January 6 certification proceeding to fraudulently alter the election results." And when that failed, on the morning of January 6, they "repeated knowingly false claims of election fraud to gathered supporters, falsely told them that the Vice President had the authority to and might alter the election results, and directed them to the Capitol to obstruct the certification proceeding." Fifth, when "a large and angry crowd . . . violently attacked the Capitol and halted the proceeding," Trump and his co-conspirators "exploited the disruption by redoubling efforts to levy false claims of election fraud and convince Members of Congress to further delay the certification."

Trump moved to dismiss the indictment, claiming absolute immunity from criminal prosecution for acts he took while president of the United States. The district court denied President Trump's motion to dismiss. Special Counsel Smith sought Supreme Court review before the matter was heard by the court of appeals. The Court denied this, and then the U.S. Court of Appeals for the District of Columbia Circuit held oral arguments. The court of appeals affirmed the district court, denying Trump immunity from prosecution. The Supreme Court granted certiorari, scheduled an additional day for oral arguments on April 25, and handed down its decision on July 1.

It was a 6–3 decision, with Chief Justice Roberts writing for the Court. Justices Thomas and Barrett each wrote concurring opinions. And Justices Sotomayor and Jackson each wrote blistering dissenting opinions.

Chief Justice Roberts's majority opinion began with the premise of a general need to protect the presidency from judicial scrutiny. He wrote: "The President occupies a unique position in the constitutional scheme, as 'the only person who alone composes a branch of government.' The Framers 'sought to encourage energetic, vigorous, decisive, and speedy execution of the laws by placing in the hands of a single, constitutionally indispensable, individual the ultimate authority that, in respect to the other branches, the Constitution divides among many.'"[20] The Court expressed concern that allowing criminal prosecutions of actions while in office could chill necessary presidential conduct: "The hesitation to execute the duties of his office fearlessly and fairly that might result when a President is making decisions under 'a pall of potential prosecution' raises 'unique risks to the effective functioning of government.'"[21] But the Court also recognized the importance of holding presidents accountable. Chief Justice Roberts observed: "The President, charged with enforcing federal criminal laws, is not above them."[22]

The Court then divided presidential acts into three categories. First, there are presidential acts carrying out official powers bestowed by the Constitution or federal statutes. For these, the president has absolute immunity from criminal prosecution. The Court said that "[w]hen the President exercises such authority, he may act even when the measures he takes are 'incompatible with the expressed or implied will of Congress.' The exclusive constitutional authority of the President 'disabl[es] the Congress from acting upon the subject.'"[23]

In this realm, Congress cannot create criminal liability: "It follows that an Act of Congress—either a specific one targeted at the President or a generally applicable one—may not criminalize the President's actions within his exclusive constitutional power. Neither may the courts adjudicate a criminal prosecution that examines such Presidential actions. We thus conclude that the President is absolutely immune from criminal prosecution for conduct within his exclusive sphere of constitutional authority."[24]

The Court was explicit that the motives of the president are irrelevant and cannot be examined by a court. The Court declared: "In dividing official from unofficial conduct, courts may not inquire into the

President's motives."[25] In fact, the Court went even further and said that evidence from these official acts could not be used to establish criminal liability in areas where the president does not have absolute immunity.

Second, there are actions that are at the "outer perimeter" of presidential powers. In this area, there is presumptive absolute immunity, but it can be overcome. The Court wrote:

> [W]e conclude that the separation of powers principles explicated in our precedent necessitate at least a *presumptive* immunity from criminal prosecution for a President's acts within the outer perimeter of his official responsibility. Such an immunity is required to safeguard the independence and effective functioning of the Executive Branch, and to enable the President to carry out his constitutional duties without undue caution.[26]

The Court did not offer a definition of what it meant by the "outer perimeter" of presidential power.

Finally, there are acts of the president that do not fit into either of these categories. Such conduct is not protected by immunity. The Court declared: "As for a President's unofficial acts, there is no immunity."[27] Toward the end of the majority opinion, the Court reiterated: "The President enjoys no immunity for his unofficial acts, and not everything the President does is official. The President is not above the law."[28] In other words, the private acts of the president, conduct that is not carrying out the powers of the office, are not safeguarded by any immunity.

The Court then opined on some of the conduct alleged in the indictment. The Court said that the president's communications with Justice Department officials are part of the president's official duties and thus are protected by absolute immunity, even if they were for the purpose of keeping the president in office. The Court said that the communications with the vice president—here the effort to persuade Vice President Mike Pence to make Trump the president—are presumptively immune, but that presumption could be overcome. The Court said that it would not opine but would remand the case concerning whether there was immunity for Trump's allegedly pressuring state election officials to find him votes and for encouraging the insurrection on January 6.

There is no doubt that the overall tone of the majority opinion was strongly supportive of absolute presidential immunity from criminal prosecution. Chief Justice Roberts concluded: "But Congress may not criminalize the President's conduct in carrying out the responsibilities of the Executive Branch under the Constitution. And the system of separated powers designed by the Framers has always demanded an energetic, independent Executive. The President therefore may not be prosecuted for exercising his core constitutional powers, and he is entitled, at a minimum, to a presumptive immunity from prosecution for all his official acts. That immunity applies equally to all occupants of the Oval Office, regardless of politics, policy, or party."[29]

Justice Thomas wrote a concurring opinion strongly endorsing absolute presidential immunity, but then went further and addressed an issue not presented by the parties: whether it violates separation of powers to have a special counsel who is appointed by the attorney general, but without specific legislative authority. Justice Thomas wrote: "[T]here are serious questions whether the Attorney General has violated that structure by creating an office of the Special Counsel that has not been established by law. Those questions must be answered before this prosecution can proceed."[30]

Justice Barrett wrote a concurring opinion that urged a narrower view of absolute presidential immunity than taken by the majority. She said that she would have the Court "assess the validity of criminal charges predicated on most official acts—*i.e.*, those falling outside of the President's core executive power—in two steps. The first question is whether the relevant criminal statute reaches the President's official conduct. Not every broadly worded statute does. If the statute covers the alleged official conduct, the prosecution may proceed only if applying it in the circumstances poses no 'dange[r] of intrusion on the authority and functions of the Executive Branch.'"[31] She described this as similar to the approach urged by the special counsel.[32]

Justice Sotomayor wrote a blistering dissent, joined by Justices Kagan and Jackson. Her first paragraph made clear her strong disagreement with the majority opinion: "Today's decision to grant former Presidents criminal immunity reshapes the institution of the Presidency. It makes a mockery of the principle, foundational to our Constitution and system of Government, that no man is above the law. Relying on little more than its own misguided wisdom about the need for 'bold and unhesitating action' by the President, the Court gives former President Trump all the immunity he asked for and more. Because our Constitution does not shield a former President from answering for criminal and treasonous acts, I dissent."[33]

Justice Sotomayor argued that there is no authority for absolute presidential immunity in the text of the Constitution or its history. The Constitution provides members of Congress immunity in the "Speech and Debate" clause, but there is no comparable provision protecting the president. She said that there is also no historical support for broad presidential immunity from criminal prosecutions. To the contrary, she says, the "historical evidence reinforces that, from the very beginning, the presumption in this Nation has always been that no man is free to flout the criminal law."[34]

Justice Sotomayor saw great dangers in according a president absolute immunity for all official acts. She declared: "The President of the United States is the most powerful person in the country, and possibly the world. When he uses his official powers in any way, under the majority's reasoning, he now will be insulated from criminal prosecution. Orders the Navy's Seal Team 6 to assassinate a political rival? Immune. Organizes a military coup to hold onto power? Immune. Takes a bribe in exchange for a pardon? Immune. Immune, immune, immune."[35] She powerfully concluded, "With fear for our democracy, I dissent."[36]

Finally, Justice Jackson also wrote a dissent that stressed the rule of law. She lamented the Court's broad scope of absolute presidential immunity from criminal prosecution. She wrote: "The Court has now declared for the first time in history that the most powerful official in the United States can (under circumstances yet to be fully determined) become a law unto himself. For my part, I simply cannot abide the majority's senseless discarding of a model of accountability for criminal acts that treats every citizen of this country as being equally subject to the law—as the Rule of Law requires."[37]

Ultimately, the majority and the dissent fundamentally disagreed over how to strike the balance between the need for presidential immunity and the need for presidential accountability. The majority strongly favored immunity; the dissent emphatically saw the need for accountability. Each side read its view into the Constitution. The majority saw the Constitution's granting authority to a president as justifying its conception of immunity. The dissent saw the checks and balances of the Constitution, the rejection of royal prerogatives, as supporting allowing liability.

The decision in *Trump v. United States* is very different from prior instances when the Court has dealt with issues of presidential accountability. In the past, when the Court has dealt with issues like this, it has been unanimous and stressed the importance of holding a president accountable and upholding the rule of law. In *United States v. Nixon*, in 1974, the Court unanimously held that President Richard Nixon could not invoke executive privilege to thwart a criminal investigation.[38] In fact, when President Gerald Ford pardoned Richard Nixon, no one suggested that a pardon was unnecessary because Nixon had absolute immunity from criminal prosecution. In *Clinton v. Jones*, in 1997, the Court unanimously ruled that President Clinton had no immunity to protect him from a lawsuit for sexual harassment that occurred when he was governor of Arkansas.[39]

But we live in a very different, far more partisan time. Indeed, the Court's handling of the case, denying review that was requested in January and then not releasing its opinion until July 1, was in itself a victory for Trump in ensuring that there is no way that Trump can be tried before the November 2024 presidential election. The Court's decision, embracing a broad view of absolute presidential immunity, is a victory for Trump and for all who will hold the presidency in the future.

Chief Justice Roberts concluded his opinion by rightly saying: "This case poses a question of lasting significance."[40] It is a case that goes to the very heart of the rule of law, which provides that no person, not even a president, is above the law.

Endnotes

1. Trump v. Anderson, 144 S. Ct. 662 (2024).
2. Trump v. United States, 144 S. Ct. 2312 (2024).
3. Anderson v. Griswold, No. 2023CV32577, 2023 WL 8006216 (Colo. Dist. Ct. Nov. 17, 2023).
4. Anderson v. Griswold, 543 P.3d 283 (Colo. 2023).
5. *Id.* at 342.
6. William Baude & Michael Stokes Paulsen, *The Sweep and Force of Section Three*, 172 U. Pa. L. Rev. 605 (2024).
7. J. Michael Luttig & Laurence H. Tribe, *Supreme Betrayal*, The Atlantic (Mar. 14, 2024), https://www.theatlantic.com/ideas/archive/2024/03/supreme-court-trump-v-anderson-fourteenth-amendment/677755/.
8. Trump v. Anderson, 144 S. Ct. 662, 671 (2024).
9. *Id.* at 667.
10. *Id.* at 668.
11. *Id.* at 670.
12. *Id.* at 671.
13. *Id.* at 670.
14. *Id.* at 672 (Sotomayor, Kagan & Jackson, JJ., concurring in the judgment).
15. *Id.* at 674.
16. *Id.*
17. *Id.* at 671 (Barrett, J., concurring and concurring in the judgment).
18. Civil Rights Cases, 3 S. Ct. 18, 20 (1883).
19. Trump v. United States, 144 S. Ct. 2312 (2024).
20. *Id.* at 2329.
21. *Id.* at 2331.
22. *Id.*
23. *Id.* at 2327.
24. *Id.* at 2329.
25. *Id.* at 2333.
26. *Id.* at 2331.
27. *Id.* at 2332.
28. *Id.* at 2347.
29. *Id.*
30. *Id.* at 2352 (Thomas, J., concurring). Two weeks after the Supreme Court's decision, a federal judge in Florida adopted Justice Thomas's reasoning and declared unconstitutional the appointment of Jack Smith as a special counsel in a criminal prosecution involving Trump's alleged mishandling of classified documents. United States v. Trump, No. 23-80101-CR-CANNON, 2024 WL 3404555 (S.D. Fla. July 15, 2024).

31. *Trump*, 144 S. Ct. at 2353 (Barrett, J., concurring).
32. *Id.*
33. *Id.* at 2355 (Sotomayor, J., dissenting).
34. *Id.* at 2359.
35. *Id.* at 2371.
36. *Id.* at 2372.
37. *Id.* at 2383 (Jackson, J., dissenting).
38. United States v. Nixon, 94 S. Ct. 3090 (1974).
39. Clinton v. Jones, 117 S. Ct. 1636 (1997).
40. *Trump*, 144 S. Ct. at 2346.

13

Voting

Two rulings of the Supreme Court during October Term 2024—one on its "shadow docket" and the other a decision on the merits—again revealed the deep division among the justices with regard to issues concerning voting and the electoral process. Each was decided by a 6–3 margin, with the familiar ideological split among the current justices, and each will have significant consequences for our political system in making it harder to bring challenges to the drawing of election districts.

Robinson v. Callais

On May 15, 2024, in *Robinson v. Callais*, the Court granted an emergency stay to litigation concerning a Voting Rights Act challenge to the drawing of congressional districts in Louisiana.[1] The result is that for the 2024 elections there will be two congressional districts in Louisiana, out of six, that have a majority Black population. With a House of Representatives that is closely divided between Democrats and Republicans, even one additional likely seat for Democrats could be decisive. Although this is at least a temporary victory for the voting rights plaintiffs, the case was 6–3, with the liberal justices in dissent.

The order issued by the Court simply said: "The applications for stay presented to JUSTICE ALITO and by him referred to the Court are granted. See Purcell v. Gonzalez, 549 U. S. 1 (2006)."[2]

Purcell v. Gonzalez (2006) was a Supreme Court order, also handed down without briefing or oral argument.[3] In *Purcell*, the federal court of appeals had found that an Arizona law requiring photo identification for voting violated the Constitution and stopped the law from going into effect. But the Supreme Court allowed the Arizona law to go into effect for the election and said, "Given the imminence of the election and the inadequate time to resolve the factual disputes, our action today shall of necessity allow the election to proceed without an injunction suspending the voter identification rules."[4]

The constitutional basis for this never has been explained by the Supreme Court. Why should unconstitutional or illegal restrictions on voting be in effect just because the challenge is being heard soon before the election? Nonetheless, the Court has invoked *Purcell v. Gonzalez* many times as establishing that federal courts cannot enjoin state and local election laws soon before an election even when the judges conclude that the Constitution is being violated.

For example, in *Republican National Committee v. Democratic National Committee* (2020), a federal district court in Wisconsin issued an order five days before the scheduled election that absentee ballots mailed and postmarked after election day, April 7, still would be counted so long as they were received by April 13.[5] The judge issued this order because of the dramatic increase in absentee ballots in April 2020 at the height of concern over the COVID-19 pandemic. Wisconsin law had previously required that ballots be received by election day. The Supreme Court overturned this order and said that extending the date by which ballots may be cast by voters for an additional six days after the scheduled election day "fundamentally alters the nature of the election."[6] The Court invoked *Purcell v. Gonzalez* and said, "This Court has repeatedly emphasized that lower federal courts should ordinarily not alter the election rules on the eve of an election."[7]

In *Allen v. Milligan*, in 2022, the Court again invoked the *Purcell* principle and stayed a ruling of a three-judge federal court that Alabama had violated the Voting Rights Act and allowed a congressional map that was found to be discriminatory to be used in the 2022 election.[8] The Court relied on *Purcell* even though it was several weeks before the primary election and many months before the general election. When the Court ultimately decided the merits in *Allen v. Milligan* in June 2023, the Court affirmed the lower court and found that Alabama had violated the Voting Rights Act.[9]

In *Robinson v. Callais*, on May 15, the three liberal justices dissented even though the effect of the Court's order was to create an additional majority Black congressional district in Louisiana. Their objection was the application and what they saw as the extension of *Purcell*. Justice Ketanji Brown Jackson wrote a dissenting opinion and explained: "In my view, *Purcell* has no role to play here. There is little risk of voter confusion from a new map being imposed this far out from the November election."[10] The concern of the dissenting justices is that the Supreme Court was extending *Purcell* from being about judicial review on the eve of an election to barring court relief even many months before the election.

Alexander v. South Carolina State Conference of the NAACP[11]

The Supreme Court has consistently held that equal protection is violated if race is used as a primary motivation in drawing election districts.[12] But the Court, in *Rucho v. Common Cause* in 2019, held that partisan gerrymandering—drawing election districts to preserve safe seats for a political party—cannot be challenged in federal court because it is a nonjusticiable political question.[13]

The problem in applying this is that there often is a strong correspondence between race and political party, as in some states Black individuals vote Democratic over 90 percent of the time. How then is it to be decided whether the election districts were based on race or party?

That was the issue in *Alexander v. South Carolina State Conference of the NAACP*, decided on May 23. A three-judge federal district court had found that race was the predominant motive in drawing congressional districts in South Carolina. The Supreme Court, in a 6–3 decision, with the majority opinion written by Justice Alito, reversed the lower court.

A three-judge federal district court held a trial and then found that the South Carolina legislature had impermissibly used race as a predominant consideration in drawing election districts. The trial court held that South Carolina drew District 1 with a 17 percent Black-voting-age population "target" in mind and that this violated the Equal Protection Clause. For similar reasons, the trial court also found that the State's putative use of race to draw District 1 unlawfully diluted the Black vote. The trial court permanently enjoined South Carolina from conducting elections in District 1 until it approved a new map.[14]

The Supreme Court found that the fact finding by the three-judge federal court was clearly erroneous and that it failed to give sufficient weight to the "presumption that the legislature acted in good faith."[15] The Court said that to demonstrate that race, rather than party, was the predominant goal in districting, "a plaintiff must prove that the State subordinated race-neutral districting criteria such as compactness, contiguity, and core preservation to 'racial considerations.'"[16]

The Court said that the lower court's decision was "clear error" because the plaintiffs "provided no direct evidence of a racial gerrymander, and their circumstantial evidence is very weak."[17] Justice Alito said that the lower court failed to "rule out the possibility that politics drove the districting process."[18] The Court explained challengers did not meet the "demanding burden" of proving that the "legislature subordinated traditional race-neutral districting principles . . . to racial considerations."[19] This was because the challengers did not provide direct evidence that the State intended to racially gerrymander the districts and because they could not offer an alternative map that would achieve the explicitly partisan goal of increasing Republican vote share while also increasing the percentage of Black voters in a district.

Justice Clarence Thomas wrote an opinion concurring in part and urged a dramatic change in the law: he would not allow equal protection challenges to election districts even on the grounds that they were impermissibly drawn to discriminate based on race. He wrote: "In my view, the Court has no power to decide these types of claims. Drawing political districts is a task for politicians, not federal judges. There are no judicially manageable standards for resolving claims about districting, and, regardless, the Constitution commits those issues exclusively to the political branches."[20] Under Justice Thomas's approach, no longer would federal courts be able to hear constitutional challenges of any type against how election districts were drawn.

Justice Elena Kagan wrote a strong dissent, joined by Justices Sonia Sotomayor and Ketanji Brown Jackson. Justice Kagan emphasized the care with which the three-judge court had considered the case over the course of a year, including a nine-day trial. The dissent objected to the majority's failure to follow the usual deferential approach to clear error review.

She said that the majority "picks and chooses evidence to its liking; ignores or minimizes less convenient proof; disdains the panel's judgments about witness credibility; and makes a series of mistakes about expert opinions . . . the proof is in the pudding: On page after page, the majority's opinion betrays its distance from, and lack of familiarity with, the events and evidence central to this case."[21] Justice Kagan lamented: "Perhaps most dispiriting is what lies behind the Court's new approach—its special rules to specially disadvantage suits to remedy race-based redistricting."[22]

Justice Kagan's concern is that the Court's decision will make it much harder to challenge the impermissible use of race in drawing election districts. She concluded her dissenting opinion: "It will be easy enough to cover your tracks in the end: Just raise a 'possibility' of non-race-based decision-making, and it will be 'dispositive.' And so this 'odious' practice of sorting citizens, built on racial generalizations and exploiting racial divisions, will continue. In the electoral sphere especially, where 'ugly patterns of pervasive racial discrimination' have so long governed, we should demand better—of ourselves, of our political representatives, and most of all of this Court."[23]

The direct implication of the case is that South Carolina can maintain its racially and partisanly gerrymandered map, which will likely ensure that the state only has one Democratic representative and six Republican representatives going forward. Justice Kagan distills the long-term consequences of the majority's decision:

> What a message to send to state legislators and mapmakers about racial gerrymandering. For reasons I've addressed, those

> actors will often have an incentive to use race as a proxy to achieve partisan ends. And occasionally they might want to straight-up suppress the electoral influence of minority voters. Go right ahead, this Court says to States today. Go ahead, though you have no recognized justification for using race, such as to comply with statutes ensuring equal voting rights. Go ahead, though you are (at best) using race as a short-cut to bring about partisan gains—to elect more Republicans in one case, more Democrats in another.[24]

Conclusion

Each of these rulings is likely to matter in the composition of the Congress that will be seated in January 2025. What these rulings have in common is that they will make it harder to bring challenges to election districts in the future. *Robinson v. Callais* will require that challenges be brought and decided much earlier to avoid the *Purcell* principle. And *Alexander v. South Carolina State Conference of the NAACP* will make it much harder to challenge election districts as impermissibly based on race.

Endnotes

1. Robinson v. Callais, 144 S. Ct. 1171 (mem.) (2024).
2. *Id.*
3. Purcell v. Gonzalez, 549 U.S. 1 (2006).
4. *Id.* at 6.
5. Republican Nat'l Comm. v. Democratic Nat'l Comm., 589 U.S. 423 (2020).
6. *Id.* at 423.
7. *Id.*
8. Merrill v. Milligan, 142 S. Ct. 879 (mem.) (2022).
9. Allen v. Milligan, 143 S. Ct. 1487 (2023).
10. Robinson v. Callais, 144 S. Ct. 1171, 1172 (2024) (Jackson, J., dissenting).
11. Alexander v. S.C. State Conf. of the NAACP, 144 S. Ct. 1221, 1237 (2024).

12. *See, e.g.*, Miller v. Johnson, 515 U.S. 900 (1995); Shaw v. Reno, 509 U.S. 630 (1993) (the use of race as a predominant factor in election districting violates equal protection).

13. Rucho v. Common Cause, 588 U.S. 684 (2019).

14. *Alexander*, 144 S. Ct. at 1238.

15. *Id.* at 1235.

16. *Id.* at 1234.

17. *Id.* at 1240.

18. *Id.* at 1243.

19. *Id.* at 1240.

20. *Id.* at 1253 (Thomas, J., concurring).

21. *Id.* at 1268–69.

22. *Id.* at 1269 (Kagan, J., dissenting).

23. *Id.*

24. *Id.* at 1286.

14

Conclusion: Looking Ahead

There now have been three terms with the Supreme Court's current six conservative justices: John Roberts, Clarence Thomas, Samuel Alito, Neil Gorsuch, Brett Kavanaugh, and Amy Coney Barrett. It is impossible to overstate how much the Court has changed the law in a relatively short period of time.

Between June 2022, when the Court released the major decisions from October Term 2021, and June 2024, the completion of October Term 2023, the Court has dramatically changed many areas of law. It overruled *Roe v. Wade* and after 49 years ended a constitutional right to abortion.[1] It has dramatically expanded gun rights and held that the only gun regulations allowed are those that existed historically.[2] It has radically changed the law concerning the religion clauses, overruling the test that had been used for over a half century for determining if there is a violation of the Establishment Clause of the First Amendment.[3] The Court ended affirmative action by colleges and universities, effectively overruling many decisions over the last 45 years.[4] The Court for the first time held that a business has a First Amendment right to violate state anti-discrimination laws when it is engaged in expressive activity.[5] The

Court has fundamentally altered the administrative state by ruling that agencies cannot act on major questions of economic or political significance without clear congressional authorization, by overruling *Chevron* deference where courts defer to agencies' interpretations of ambiguous statutes, and by holding that agencies cannot impose civil penalties.[6] The Court has broadly granted the president immunity from criminal prosecution for anything done carrying out the president's constitutional or statutory duties.[7]

It is striking that each of these decisions was 6–3 (although Chief Justice Roberts only concurred in the judgment in overruling *Roe*). And each of these decisions moved the law in a much more conservative direction. They are entirely the product of the 2016 presidential election and President Donald Trump having been able to appoint three justices to the Court. If Hillary Clinton had been elected in 2016 and if she instead had appointed the three justices, none of these cases would have been decided the same way.

What should we expect from the Court in October Term 2024? What should we expect beyond that?

October Term 2024

Before the justices adjourned for their summer recess, they granted review in 28 cases, filling their argument calendars for October, November, and most of December 2024. From late September through January, they will continue to take cases to be heard and decided next term. They again are on pace to decide around 60 cases or a bit less. Here are some of the cases that are most likely to be significant where review was granted before the summer recess.

United States v. Skrmetti involves a Tennessee law that prohibits gender-affirming care for transgender minors.[8] In 2023, Tennessee passed Senate Bill 1, which prohibits healthcare provided for

> (A) Enabling a minor to identify with, or live as, a purported identity inconsistent with the minor's sex; or

> (B) Treating purported discomfort or distress from a discordance between the minor's sex and asserted identity.[9]

Three transgender teenagers, all receiving gender-affirming care, filed a lawsuit seeking to enjoin enforcement of SB 1. The Biden administration joined the lawsuit on behalf of the plaintiffs.

The district court issued a ruling that prevented implementation of SB 1 until litigation had concluded, finding that "parents have a fundamental right to direct the medical care of their children, which naturally includes the right of parents to request certain medical treatments on behalf of their children."[10] Additionally, the district court found discrimination on the basis of gender identity and that the plaintiffs were likely to prevail on their equal protection claims. The court used intermediate scrutiny and powerfully concluded:

> The Court acknowledges that the state feels strongly that the medical procedures banned by SB1 are harmful to minors. The medical evidence on the record, however, indicates otherwise. It is undisputed that every major medical organization to take a position on the issue, which includes the AAP, American Medical Association, American Psychiatric Association, American Psychological Association, and American Academy of Child Adolescent Psychiatry, agrees that puberty blockers and cross-sex hormone therapy are appropriate and medically necessary treatments for adolescents when clinically indicated. It is of little surprise, therefore, that all major medical organizations oppose outright bans on gender-affirming medical care for adolescents with gender dysphoria.[11]

Therefore, "the Court finds that at this juncture, SB1 is not supported by an important state interest."[12] However, the district court did not rule on the issue of gender-transition surgeries because none of the plaintiffs sought those operations.[13]

The U.S. Court of Appeals for the Sixth Circuit simultaneously evaluated Tennessee and Kentucky laws prohibiting gender-affirming care for transgender minors. It reversed the preliminary injunctions from the lower courts, upholding the laws. The court cited studies from the late 1970s and early 1980s that recommended only adults undergo hormonal and surgical treatments for "gender dysphoria" (the terminology used throughout the case).[14]

The court urged deference to the political process. First, "judges should be wary of removing a vexing and novel topic of medical debate from the ebbs and flows of democracy"; second, "[c]onstitutionalizing new areas of American life is not something federal courts should do lightly"; and third, "[s]tates are indeed engaged in thoughtful debates over this issue. . . . Failure to allow these laws to go into effect would start to grind these all-over-the-map gears to a halt."[15]

The court rejected the due process claims and as to equal protection said that the "Tennessee and Kentucky laws treat similarly situated individuals evenhandedly. And that is true however one characterizes the alleged classifications in the law, whether as premised on age, medical condition, or sex."[16] The Sixth Circuit rejected the argument that discrimination against transgender individuals warrants heightened scrutiny.

The Supreme Court granted review on the question of whether the Tennessee law violates equal protection.[17] The case will matter for transgender youth in the United States. "As of May 2024, 39% or 117,600 trans youth aged 13-17 are living in the 25 states that have passed bans on gender-affirming care."[18] A number of conservative states have adopted laws like Tennessee's, and this case will likely determine the fate of those statutes. This case will also likely see the Supreme Court address the level of scrutiny that will apply to discrimination against transgender individuals and whether they are to be treated as a "suspect class." It is a case that once more puts the Supreme Court squarely in the middle of the "culture wars."

Garland v. Vanderstock involves the legality of a federal regulation prohibiting ghost guns—privately produced guns without serial numbers.[19] The case concerns a 2022 Bureau of Alcohol, Tobacco, and Firearms (ATF) regulation that sought to regulate "ghost guns."[20] Under the Gun Control Act (GCA), the federal government imposes criminal penalties on individuals who sell "firearms" without a license. The ATF defined this term in 1978, but the 2021 revisions sought to regulate "privately made firearms" (PMFs). These PMFs, also known colloquially as "ghost guns," are often made from readily purchasable "firearm parts kits, standalone frame or receiver parts, and easy-to-complete frames or receivers."[21] Because the kits and standalone parts were not themselves considered "firearms" under any interpretation of the GCA and ATF's related definitions, manufacturers of such kits are neither subject to licensing requirements nor required to conduct background checks on purchasers. Further, when made for personal use, PMFs "are not required by the GCA to have a serial number placed on the frame or receiver." These facts, ATF contends, make PMFs attractive to criminal actors and "pose a challenge to law enforcement's ability to investigate crimes."[22]

The district court issued preliminary injunctions blocking the implementation of the ATF rule and then issued summary judgment for the plaintiffs, vacating the ATF rule. The U.S. Court of Appeals for the Fifth Circuit ruled against the government, concluding that "[t]he agency rule at issue here flouts clear statutory text and exceeds the legislatively-imposed limits on agency authority in the name of public policy. Because Congress has neither authorized the expansion of firearm regulation nor permitted the criminalization of previously lawful conduct, the proposed rule constitutes unlawful agency action, in direct contravention of the legislature's will."[23]

Like *Garland v. Cargill*,[24] the October Term 2023 case concerning government regulation of bump stocks, this case about ghost guns does not involve the Second Amendment. Rather, it is about whether an action of the federal government regulating guns had sufficient statutory authorization. Though there certainly is a compelling law enforcement need to regulate ghost guns, this case arises before a Court that is often sympathetic to gun rights.

Glossip v. Oklahoma.[25] The Court has not decided a major death penalty case in several years. In 2004, Richard Glossip was convicted of first-degree murder by a jury in Oklahoma County District Court. When Glossip was originally convicted and sentenced, the State relied on its "indispensable witness," Justin Sneed. However, it has now become clear that Justin Sneed in fact murdered the victim.[26] After the State solicited information from Sneed accusing Glossip, it "allowed Sneed to affirmatively tell the jury he had not seen a psychiatrist," even though a doctor had said he had "a psychiatric condition that rendered him volatile and 'potentially violent,' particularly when combined with methamphetamine use, a street drug Sneed was abusing at the time."[27]

Glossip repeatedly appealed his sentencing, to no avail. In fact, Glossip's case came to the Supreme Court in 2015, when the Court upheld the use of lethal injections using midazolam to execute prisoners, unless the condemned individual can provide a known and available alternative that would inflict substantially less pain.[28]

Subsequently, information was discovered indicating the State had wrongly convicted Glossip. Indeed, the State of Oklahoma confessed error, admitting that the failure to disclose the truth about Sneed's psychiatric condition, leaving the jury with Sneed's uncorrected false testimony and then suppressing this information for a quarter century, rendered "Glossip's trial unfair and unreliable."[29] "Before this Court, the State has admitted Mr. Glossip is entitled to a new trial on these grounds, as well as in light of 'cumulative error' regarding 'multiple issues raised in Glossip's Post-Conviction Relief Application.'"[30]

But the Oklahoma Court of Criminal Appeals has refused to stop the execution. The U.S. Supreme Court granted review of several questions, including "[w]hether the State's suppression of the key prosecution witness's admission he was under the care of a psychiatrist and failure to correct that witness's false testimony about that care and related diagnosis violate the due process of law." Also, the Court granted review on "whether due process of law requires reversal, where a capital conviction is so infected with errors that the State no longer seeks to defend it." In addition, the parties were directed to brief whether the Oklahoma Court of Criminal Appeals' holding that the Oklahoma Post-Conviction Procedure Act precluded post-conviction relief is an adequate and independent state-law ground for the judgment.[31]

This is likely to be an important case for precedent regarding the death penalty. Will the Supreme Court allow an innocent person to be sentenced to death, even when the State now agrees that man should not be executed? What is the legal effect of the State of Oklahoma confessing error? The case also poses important issues about the government's duties under *Brady* and when a state law ground is an independent and adequate state law ground of decision.

Seven County Infrastructure Coalition v. Eagle County, Colorado.[32] This case has the potential for important implications for energy project development and environmental law generally. It involves the National Environmental Policy Act, a cornerstone of federal environmental law, which requires federal agencies to assess the environmental effects of their proposed actions prior to making decisions.

In *Department of Transportation v. Public Citizen* (2004), the Supreme Court ruled that when an agency cannot prevent an environmental effect "due to its limited statutory authority over the relevant actions," the National Environmental Policy Act (NEPA) does not require it to study that effect.[33] The circuits are split over how to interpret and implement this. In this case, the Surface Transportation Board relied on the Court's decision in *Public Citizen* to limit its environmental review of a new rail line in Utah. But the U.S. Court of Appeals for the District of Columbia Circuit rejected that approach, ruling that the Board "cannot avoid" environmental review "on the ground that it lacks authority to prevent, control, or mitigate" distant environmental effects. As a result, it ordered the Board to study the local effects of oil wells and refineries that lie outside the Board's regulatory authority.[34] The court's opinion focused on how "the EIS [Environmental Impact Statement] failed to demonstrate that the Board took the requisite 'hard look' at all of the environmental impacts of the Railway."[35]

The Supreme Court granted review on the question of "[w]hether the National Environmental Policy Act requires an agency to study environmental impacts beyond the proximate effects of the action over which the agency has regulatory authority." The case could be very important in defining the scope of NEPA and also in focusing on how to determine causation in its implementation.

Royal Canin USA v. Wullschleger.[36] If a case is removed from state court to federal court and the plaintiff amends the complaint to dismiss all of the federal claims, does that defeat federal court jurisdiction?

Anastasia Wullschleger filed a class action suit against Royal Canin and Nestle Purina in state court for selling prescription dog food that contained no medications. Her suit alleged that the prescription requirement is misleading because the Food and Drug Administration never actually evaluates the product. The lawsuit sought damages for the higher sales price that resulted from requiring that the dog food be bought by prescription.[37]

Royal Canin and Nestle Purina removed the case to federal court. When the case was in federal district court, Wullschleger amended her complaint and "eliminated every reference to federal law in the complaint, cut the antitrust and unjust-enrichment claims, and narrowed her request for injunctive relief. As a replacement, she added a civil-conspiracy claim."[38] The district court nonetheless found that federal question jurisdiction still existed.

The U.S. Court of Appeals for the Eighth Circuit reversed and held that the amended complaint did not provide a basis for federal jurisdiction: "[T]here is nothing federal about it."[39] The Eighth Circuit also said that there was not a basis for supplemental jurisdiction because there are no longer any federal claims. The court explained: "The original complaint is 'without legal effect,' meaning that the possibility of supplemental jurisdiction vanished right alongside the once-present federal questions."[40] The court of appeals remanded the case to state court.

The Supreme Court granted certiorari on two questions:

1. Whether such a post-removal amendment of the complaint defeats federal-question subject-matter jurisdiction.
2. Whether such a post-removal amendment of the complaint precludes a district court from exercising supplemental jurisdiction over the plaintiff's remaining state-law claims pursuant to 28 U.S.C. § 1367.

This case feels like it was custom built for a Civil Procedure final. It involves federal-question jurisdiction, removal, amended complaints, and more. The decision is likely to provide clarification of issues that frequently arise in federal court litigation.

Williams v. Washington. If I were to pick a potential sleeper case for the term, it would be *Williams v. Washington*, which poses the question of "[w]hether exhaustion of state administrative remedies is required to bring claims under 42 U.S.C. § 1983 in state court."[41]

The Supreme Court has consistently held that there is not an exhaustion requirement before bringing Section 1983 claims. In 1963, in *McNeese v. Board of Education*, the Court considered an Illinois administrative remedy for segregated public schools.[42] Under an Illinois statute, whenever at least 50 residents believed a school district to be segregated, they could file a complaint with the superintendent of public instruction. The superintendent then would hold a hearing on the matter. If they found the complaint to be "substantially correct," the superintendent would request the attorney general to file suit. The superintendent's request did not obligate the attorney general to initiate litigation.

The plaintiffs in *McNeese* filed suit in federal court without using the state's administrative scheme. The state moved for dismissal on the ground that the plaintiffs were required to exhaust their state administrative remedies before suing under Section 1983. The Court disagreed. The Court held that "relief under the Civil Rights Act may not be defeated because relief was not first sought under state law which provided a remedy."[43] The Court based its conclusion on the legislative history of Section 1983. The statute was passed, the Court argued, to "provide a remedy where state law was inadequate . . . and to provide a remedy in the federal courts supplementary to any remedy any State might have."[44] To require exhaustion of state remedies would subvert that goal.

On several occasions, the Supreme Court reiterated its conclusion that plaintiffs need not exhaust state administrative remedies before initiating federal court Section 1983 litigation.[45] In 1982, in *Patsy v. Board of Regents*, the Court reconsidered the exhaustion issue.[46] Once again, the Court concluded that "exhaustion of state administrative remedies should not be required as a prerequisite to bringing an action pursuant to section 1983."[47]

In *Patsy*, the plaintiff filed an employment discrimination claim alleging that her employer, Florida International University, had denied her employment opportunities on account of her race and gender. The State of Florida provided an administrative remedy for employment discrimination claims against state agencies. The Court reiterated its position that the legislative history of Section 1983 reveals Congress's intent that plaintiffs need not exhaust state remedies before filing federal civil rights litigation. The Court stated that Section 1983 granted the federal courts a "paramount role in protecting constitutional rights."[48]

More recently, in 2019, in *Knick v. Township of Scott, Pennsylvania*, the Court held that there is no need to exhaust state administrative or judicial remedies before bringing a takings claim under Section 1983.[49] Earlier the Court had ruled that takings claims were not ripe until compensation has been sought and denied through the available administrative procedures. But in *Knick*, the Court, 5–4, reversed these decisions and stated: "A property owner has an actionable Fifth Amendment takings claim when the government takes his property without paying for it."[50] The Court said that there was no reason to treat takings claims differently from other constitutional rights.

Williams v. Washington arose when Nancy Williams sued under Section 1983 in Alabama state court, complaining about delays in the processing of unemployment benefits. The Alabama Supreme Court affirmed the trial court's dismissal of the case, holding that the Alabama "Legislature has prohibited courts from exercising jurisdiction over the plaintiffs' claims at this stage" before the claimants had exhausted their administrative remedies.[51]

If the Supreme Court were to affirm the Alabama Supreme Court, it would be a dramatic change in what the law has been for over a half century. For example, it would require the Court to reconsider its recent holding in *Knick* that exhaustion is not required in order to bring a takings claim. Conceivably, the Court could distinguish many of the prior cases by saying exhaustion is not required before a federal court suit under Section 1983, but it is for a state court suit under Section 1983. But since the Court's reasoning has been that an exhaustion requirement is inconsistent with Section 1983, it does not seem that the forum should matter.

Looking to the Future

When the Court begins October Term 2024 on Monday, October 7, it will be the third year with the current nine justices. As the Court starts the new term, Justice Clarence Thomas will be the oldest justice at 76. The other justices in age order are Samuel Alito, 74; Sonia Sotomayor, 70; John Roberts, 69; Elena Kagan, 64; Brett Kavanaugh, 59; Neil Gorsuch, 57; Ketanji Brown Jackson, 54; and Amy Coney Barrett, 52.

It is easy to imagine this group of justices being together for another decade. Yet, it also is easy to imagine that if Donald Trump is elected president in November 2024 and there is a Republican Senate, Justices Thomas and Alito might retire to allow appointment of young conservatives who will keep their seats occupied by conservatives for decades to come. Likewise, if Kamala Harris is elected and there is a Democratic Senate, it is easy to imagine Justice Sotomayor stepping down.

Thus, even though no vacancies on the Court are imminent, there is no doubt that the presidential election could matter greatly for the future composition of the Supreme Court. One of the longest-lasting legacies of any presidency are the justices and federal judges picked for lifetime appointments. Virtually every major case decided this term, and reviewed in this book, would have come out differently if Hillary Clinton had been elected in 2016 rather than Donald Trump.

Endnotes

1. Dobbs v. Jackson Women's Health Org., 597 U.S. 215 (2022).
2. N.Y. State Rifle & Pistol Ass'n, Inc. v. Bruen, 597 U.S. 1 (2022); United States v. Rahimi, 144 S. Ct. 1889 (2024).
3. Kennady v. Bremerton Sch. Dist., 597 U.S. 507 (2022).
4. Students for Fair Admissions, Inc. v. President & Fellows of Harvard Coll., 600 U.S. 181 (2023).
5. 303 Creative LLC v. Elenis, 600 U.S. 570 (2023).
6. West Virginia v. Env't Prot. Agency, 597 U.S. 697 (2022); Biden v. Nebraska, 143 S. Ct. 2355 (2023); Loper Bright Enters. v. Raimondo, 144 S. Ct. 2244 (2024); Sec. & Exch. Comm'n v. Jarkesy, 144 S. Ct. 2117 (2024).
7. Trump v. United States, 144 S. Ct. 2312 (2024).
8. United States v. Skrmetti, No. 23-477 (cert. granted June 24, 2024), https://www.supremecourt.gov/qp/23-00477qp.pdf.
9. Tenn. Code § 68-33-103.
10. L.W. v. Skrmetti, 679 F. Supp. 3d 668, 684 (M.D. Tenn. 2023).
11. *Id.* at 709.
12. *Id.*
13. *Id.* at 681.
14. L.W. v. Skrmetti, 83 F.4th 460, 466–67 (6th Cir. 2023).

15. *Id.*

16. *Id.* at 479.

17. Lackey v. Stinnie, No. 23-621 (cert. granted Apr. 22, 2024), https://www.supremecourt.gov/qp/23-00621qp.pdf.

18. HRC Found., *Map: Attacks on Gender Affirming Care by State*, Hum. Rights Campaign, https://www.hrc.org/resources/attacks-on-gender-affirming-care-by-state-map (last visited Aug. 13, 2024).

19. Garland v. Vanderstok, No. 23-852 (cert. granted Apr. 22, 2024), https://www.supremecourt.gov/qp/23-00852qp.pdf.

20. Definition of "Frame or Receiver" and Identification of Firearms, 87 Fed. Reg. 24,652 (Apr. 26, 2022), https://www.federalregister.gov/documents/2022/04/26/2022-08026/definition-of-frame-or-receiver-and-identification-of-firearms.

21. *Id.*

22. *Id.* at 24,658.

23. VanDerStok v. Garland, 86 F.4th 179, 182 (5th Cir. 2023).

24. Garland v. Cargill, 602 U.S. 406 (2024) (discussed in Chapter 10).

25. Glossip v. Oklahoma, No. 22-7466 (cert. granted Jan. 22, 2024), https://www.supremecourt.gov/qp/22-07466qp.pdf.

26. *Id.*

27. *Id.*

28. Glossip v. Gross, 576 U.S. 863 (2015).

29. Glossip v. Oklahoma, No. 22-7466 (cert. granted Jan. 22, 2024), https://www.supremecourt.gov/qp/22-07466qp.pdf.

30. *Id.*

31. *Id.*

32. Seven Cnty. Infrastructure Coal. v. Eagle Cnty., Colo., No. 23-975 (cert. granted June 24, 2024), https://www.supremecourt.gov/qp/23-00975qp.pdf.

33. Dep't of Transp. v. Pub. Citizen, 541 U.S. 752 (2004).

34. Seven Cnty. Infrastructure Coal. v. Eagle Cnty., Colo., No. 23-975 (cert. granted June 24, 2024), https://www.supremecourt.gov/qp/23-00975qp.pdf.

35. Eagle Cnty. v. Surface Transp. Bd., 82 F.4th 1152, 1175 (D.C. Cir. 2023).

36. Royal Canin U.S.A., Inc. v. Wullschleger, No. 23-677 (cert. granted Mar. 29, 2024), https://www.supremecourt.gov/qp/23-00677qp.pdf.

37. Wullschleger v. Royal Canin U.S.A., Inc., 75 F.4th 918 (8th Cir. 2023).

38. *Id.* at 921.

39. *Id.* at 922.

40. *Id.* at 924.

41. Williams v. Washington, No. 23-191 (cert. granted Jan. 12, 2024), https://www.supremecourt.gov/qp/23-00191qp.pdf.

42. McNeese v. Bd. of Educ., 373 U.S. 668 (1963).

43. *Id.* at 671.

44. *Id.* at 672.

45. *See, e.g.*, King v. Smith, 392 U.S. 309 (1968); Houghton v. Shafer, 392 U.S. 639 (1968); Damico v. California, 389 U.S. 416 (1967).

46. Patsy v. Bd. of Regents, 457 U.S. 496 (1982).

47. *Id.* at 516.

48. *Id.* at 503.

49. Knick v. Twp. of Scott, Pa., 139 S. Ct. 2162 (2019). *Knick* is discussed in § 2.4 to its implications for ripeness.

50. *Id.* at 2167.

51. Johnson v. Ala. Sec. of Lab. Fitzgerald Washington, No. SC-2022-0897, 2023 WL 4281620, at *1 (Ala. June 30, 2023).

Index

www.ingramcontent.com/pod-product-compliance
Lightning Source LLC
LaVergne TN
LVHW022045200926
848481LV00003B/795